basic
PROJECTS

Dreamweaver
CS3

> John Giles

www.payne-gallway.co.uk

✓ Free online support
✓ Useful weblinks
✓ 24 hour online ordering

01865 888070

PAYNE-GALLWAY

Payne-Gallway is an imprint of Pearson Education Limited, a company incorporated in England and Wales, having its registered office at Edinburgh Gate, Harlow, Essex, CM20 2JE. Registered company number: 872828

www.payne-gallway.co.uk

Text © John Giles 2008

First published 2008

12 11 10 09 08
10 9 8 7 6 5 4 3 2 1

British Library Cataloguing in Publication Data
A catalogue record for this book is available from the British Library

ISBN 978 1 905292 47 9

Designed by Wooden Ark Studios
Edited and typeset by Sparks Publishing Services Ltd – www.sparkspublishing.com
Cover design by Wooden Ark Studios
Printed in Great Britain by Scotprint

Acknowledgements
Every effort has been made to contact copyright holders of material reproduced in this book. Any omissions will be rectified in subsequent printings if notice is given to the publishers.

Original Slurp can design by Frances Sharp

Websites
The websites used in this book were correct and up-to-date at the time of publication. It is essential for tutors to preview each website before using it in class so as to ensure that the URL is still accurate, relevant and appropriate. We suggest that tutors bookmark useful websites and consider enabling students to access them through the school/college intranet.

Ordering Information
Payne-Gallway, FREEPOST (OF1771),
PO Box 381, Oxford OX2 8BR
Tel: 01865 888070
Fax: 01865 314029
Email: orders@payne-gallway.co.uk

CONTENTS

So you know ...

Dreamweaver is one of many applications that are used to produce websites. Some applications designed for this purpose require you to write the instructions for the design of a website in a code such as HTML, which stands for Hyper Text Markup Language. This means you would need to learn the code and how to use it before you can make even the simplest website.

Fortunately for us, Dreamweaver looks after writing the code while we get on with designing the site using screen editing techniques that are similar to desktop publishing.

It's hard to avoid using websites now as so many of our everyday tasks are done over the Internet – there are an incredible number of websites to access and they all have to be built and published on the web. Some websites are much more complex than others, but the following pages will give you the basics on how to build your own.

You will first learn some of the skills needed to use Dreamweaver and then you will be asked to make decisions about the kinds of website features needed for a particular audience and purpose. This will allow you to show your capability in using ICT and achieve higher National Curriculum levels.

The skills that you will learn are:

Task 1: How to build pages for a website
Task 2: How to link pages in a website
Task 3: How to animate features on a website

Once you have completed the three Tasks, you are going to use the skills that you have learnt to carry out the final Project. You are eventually going to produce a website to help the sixth form to run their 'Break Bites' snack ordering service. When you have learned the skills to create everything you'll need, it will be up to you to decide how to use your skills to create the look and feel of your website.

FIgure Intro.1 shows Dreamweaver in use:

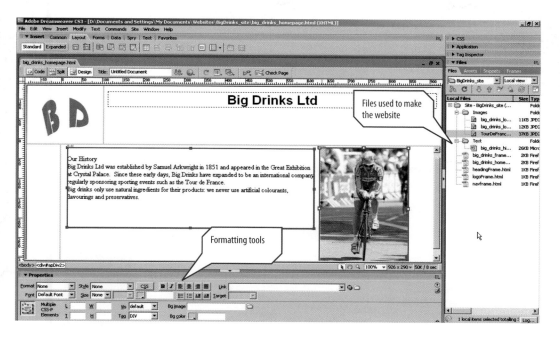

Figure Intro.1

This book also helps you to develop your Functional Skills in ICT. This is all about you being able to use your software skills in the way that best suits the activity that you have been given – in other words *why* you are doing something in the way that you have chosen. For example, you always need to be thinking about the purpose of what you are doing – what has it got to do with the project, what kind of impact do you want to achieve, who is going to see or use what you're working on, i.e. who is your audience, and what is the background of the situation – for example do you need to produce a formal or informal document? By considering all of these things you should be able to produce the right kind of documents that are 'fit for purpose', i.e. they do the job they need to do. A lot to take in at once I know, but have a look at the Functional Skills tabs as you work through the book and they'll show you what all this means in practice… so that you can use them to help you with your project.

Before we start with Task 1, though, the next few pages show you some of the most important skills that you'll need throughout your whole project: how to start the program, create new files and save your work. Remember that you can return to these pages to remind yourself of these skills if you forget later on in the project.

FUNCTIONAL SKILLS

Choosing the best software to meet your needs means that your task will be completed in the most efficient and effective way – in this example we have chosen Dreamweaver because it is the best software package available to us for building websites

STARTING DREAMWEAVER

Either:

1 Click on **Start**.

2 Click **All Programs**.

3 Select **Adobe Dreamweaver CS3**.

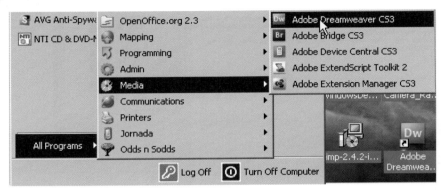

Figure Intro.2

Or just double click the DW icon on the desktop:

FINDING YOUR WAY AROUND

Let's have a look at the welcome screen as Dreamweaver loads.

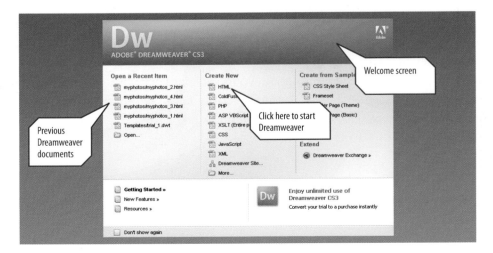

Figure Intro.3

This screen gives you access to previous Dreamweaver files, but if you are starting afresh you will probably not see any files here.

1 In the **Create New** panel, click **HTML**.

The welcome screen disappears, and the main application window loads and is shown on the screen. Spend a few minutes to compare Figure Intro.4 with your own screen, so that you can identify the parts:

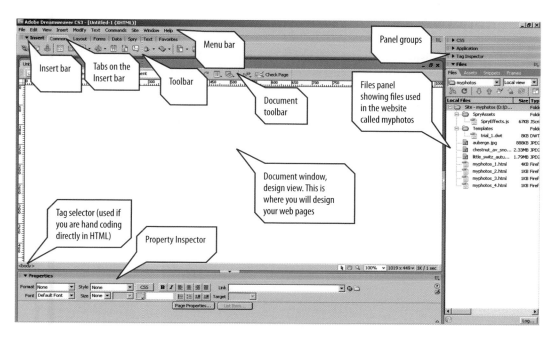

Figure Intro.4

As well as this 'design view' there is a code view, which is used for 'hand coding' web pages – this is where you could type HTML code.

2 Click **Code** on the **Document** toolbar.

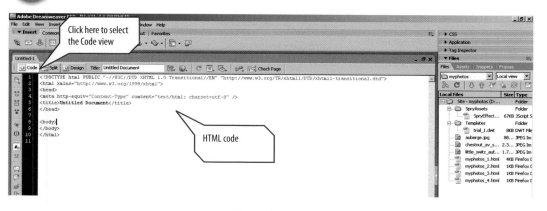

Figure Intro.5

There is also a **Split** view, which gives a view of the design and code. This is not very convenient to use unless you have a large monitor screen.

GETTING STARTED

You don't have to start from scratch! Dreamweaver has a selection of already-formed pages that you can use in your website, although mainly you will only want to use these as a start as you'll want to add your own ideas to them as well.

Depending on the amount of help you want at the start, you can select:

➤ **Blank Page**. This allows you to choose from several different layouts but doesn't format the contents.

➤ **Blank Template**. This allows you to choose a style (template) for the whole of your website. This is useful because if you want to change the style then all of the pages in the website can be changed at once as they're based on the same template.

➤ **Page from Template**. If you have already created a site using a template this option allows you to add more pages to it using the same template.

➤ **Page from Sample**. This allows you to choose from several different layouts and some formatting options for the content. Have a look at Figure Intro.6, which shows a list of layout options.

Let's have a look at some.

 Right click on the tab 'Untitled-1' (see Figure Intro.5) and select **New Document**.

The New Document dialogue box loads:

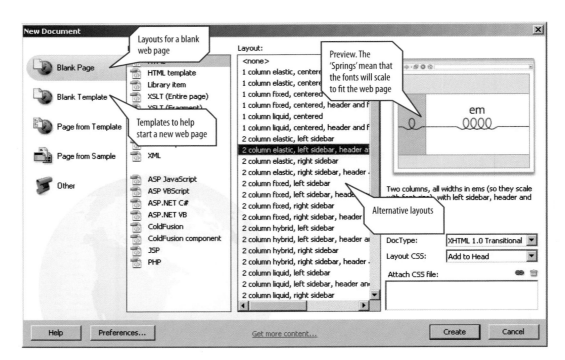

Figure Intro.6

4 Choose (click) the **Page from Sample** option.

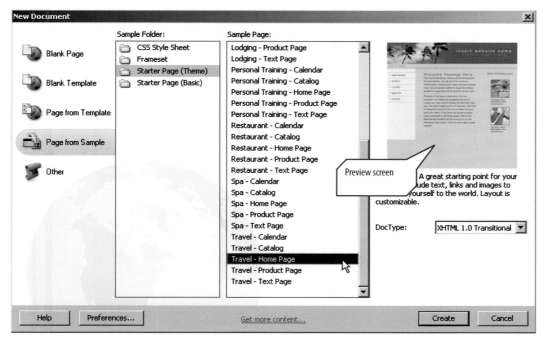

Figure Intro.7

5 Select (click) **Starter Page (Theme)**.

6 Select (click) **Travel – Home Page**.

7 Click the **Create** button.

You will be prompted to save the new web page. You should *always* create a new folder structure for each website because by the end, when you have many pages and images, you'll have lots of files so you need to make sure they're well organised from the start.

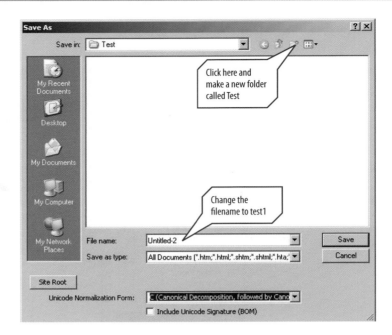

Figure Intro.8

In this case we will create a folder called Test and store the file as test1.

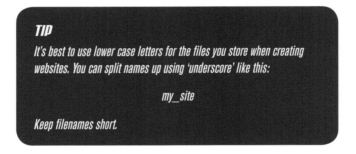

The **Copy Dependent Files** dialogue box loads:

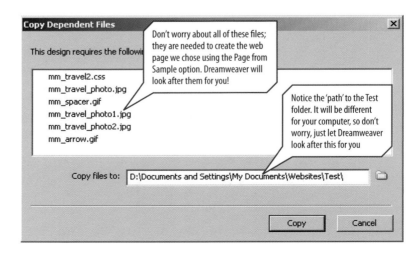

Figure Intro.9

 Click **Copy**.

You will see this screen:

Figure Intro.10

It is often useful to be able to see what your web page will look like once it is on the web. This also checks that it will work, which is pretty useful too!

 Look in the **Document** toolbar and find the **Preview/Debug in browser** button.

 Click this button. Then choose the browser that you use to explore the Internet:

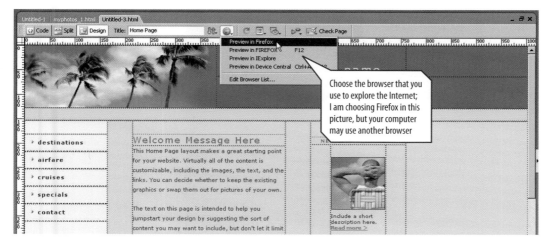

Figure Intro.11

Figure Intro.12

 11 Close the browser by clicking the cross in the top-right corner.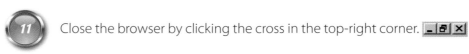

We will practise saving the page, although we will not use it again.

 12 Click on **File** in the menu bar, then click **Save As**.

Figure Intro.13

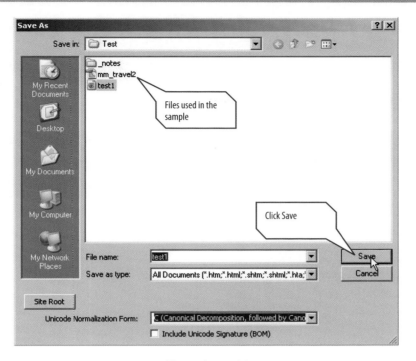

Figure Intro.14

 14 Click **Save**.

 15 Close Dreamweaver by clicking on the cross at the top right of the screen. ▃⧉✕

GET AHEAD

In Task 1 you will design a website for a soft drinks manufacturer called Big Drinks Ltd. Big Drinks produce many soft drinks, the most recent of which is called 'Slurp'.

The company needs a new website to provide a catalogue of products that are already available and more detailed information on their new product Slurp. The website should also provide customers with contact details so that shops stocking Big Drinks products can buy them online.

Make a flying start on this task by completing the following questions:

 1 Who is the target audience?

 2 Make a list of the information that your audience will want to find on the website.

 3 Use the following table to show how you would organise the information that will be shown on your website:

Page	Suggested page layout (drawing)	Links (draw arrows)
Home page		
Products page		
Slurp page		

THIRSTY WORK ON THE WEB

TASK BRIEF

Big Drinks Ltd is a manufacturer of soft drinks, including their most recent drink, 'Slurp'. The company needs a new website and they're looking for a design company to build it for them. The website will be used by shops and other businesses to view and order Big Drinks' products to sell in their own stores.

BRIEF

Big Drinks require the new website to have the following pages:

➤ Home page: this should include the name of the company, contact details, and logo.

➤ Products page: this should advertise and give information about Big Drinks products already on sale.

➤ Slurp page: this should advertise their latest product, Slurp.

As you create the website, you will cover the following:

SOFTWARE SKILLS

You will learn how to:

> *Set up a root folder*

> *Use frames*

> *Save files*

> *Add content to frames (images and text)*

FUNCTIONAL SKILLS

As you work through this task the Functional Skills tabs will explain to you why the decisions have been made to respond to the brief in the way shown in Task 1 and explain why you would choose to:

> *Plan and design web pages*

> *Organise files*

> *Test the website*

CAPABILITY

You will show capability in the following if you do not follow the instructions exactly as shown in Task 1:

> Matching your home page layout to your audience's needs

VOCABULARY

You should learn these new words and understand what they mean:

> Internet

> Website

> Web page

> Web browser

> Frame

> Root folder

> URL

RESOURCES

There are four files for this task that you should download from www.payne-gallway.co.uk

Big Drinks Ltd logos:
big_drinks_logo1.jpg
big_drinks_logo2.jpg

Image: TourDeFrance_1.jpg

Text: Big_drinks_history.doc

 TARGET POINT

Turn the page to see your Target Points for this task.

	Level 3	Level 4	Level 5	Level 6
	You have followed the instructions to set up the root folder	You have successfully set up the root folder	You have worked unaided to set up the root folder	
	You have used navigation techniques to locate the necessary files	You have copied the files to a new location	You have shown that you understand the need to store files needed for the website in the root folder	
	You have used frames	You have successfully set up frames in the website		You have understood the relation between frame files stored in the root folder and the frame structure of the website
	You have inserted text from a text file	You have used an AP element to contain the text	You have successfully arranged the AP element on the web page	
	You have inserted an image from an image file	You have used an AP element to contain an image	You have successfully arranged the AP element on the web page	
	You have inserted a table	You have used an AP element to contain the table	You have successfully arranged the AP element on the web page	
	You have performed a test to make sure that the website works correctly	You have carried out a test without seeking help	You understand why the tests are necessary and have carried out tests in more than one browser	
	You have saved your work	You have saved your work using appropriate filenames		

We're going to look at how we build the home page.

OK, let's get started.

STEP 1: CREATING A LOCAL ROOT FOLDER

Unlike a word-processed letter written in Word or a spreadsheet in Excel, which usually consist of one file, a website consists of many files. Files are made for every picture in the website, page of text and animation, so even quite small websites can contain many files.

It's important to realise that, for the website to function, Dreamweaver has to know where you have stored each file. Finding them is made easy though – Dreamweaver does this for you!

This is where the 'local root folder' comes in: it is the place where all your files for a website are stored, allowing Dreamweaver to locate each file easily as required.

We will make a local root folder for a website for Big Drinks Ltd.

Load Dreamweaver. The welcome screen appears:

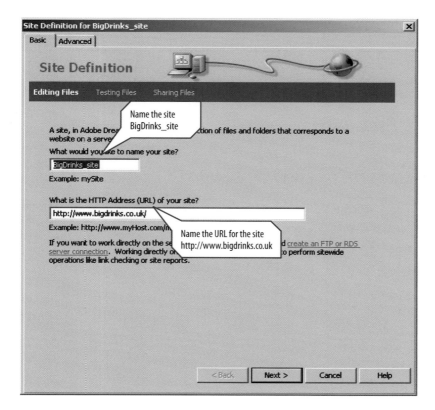

Figure 1.1

The **Site Definition** wizard loads:

Figure 1.2

We are not ready to put the site on the web yet, but just fill in the URL box as if we were about to publish the site on the Internet.

 Click **Next** and choose the first option.

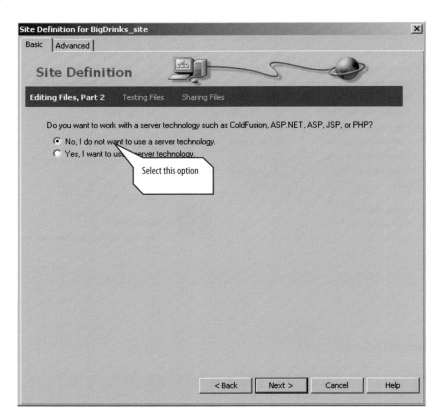

Figure 1.3

 Click **Next**.

 Click on the first option.

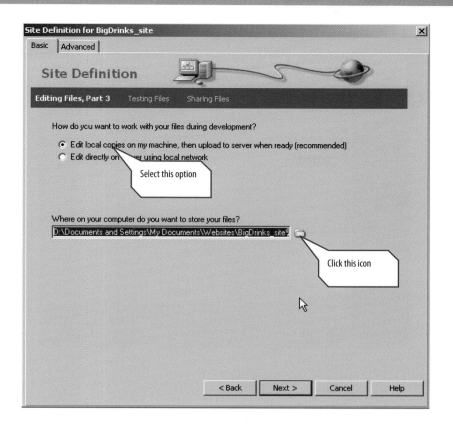

Figure 1.4

 Click the **Folder** icon to choose where on your computer you want to save your files.

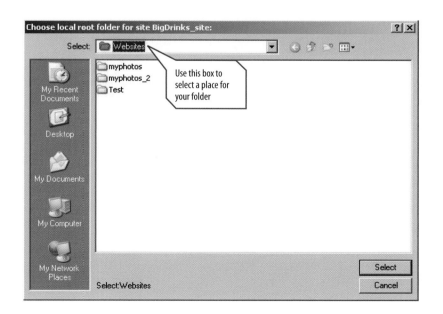

Figure 1.5

6 Once you have chosen a suitable location, create a new folder and rename it as shown. Once the folder is renamed, the **Open** button changes to **Select**.

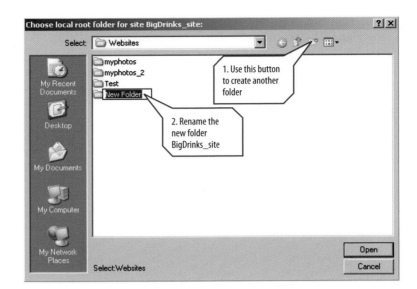

Figure 1.6

7 Click **Select**.

The **Site Definition** wizard reappears.

8 Click **Next**.

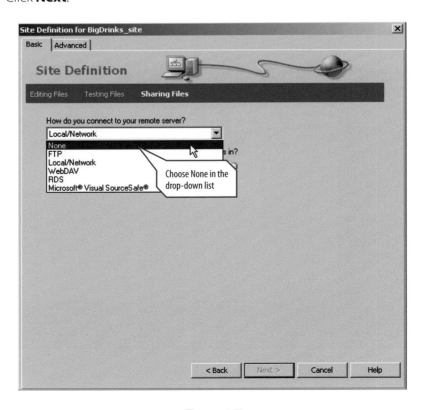

Figure 1.7

9 Choose **None** from the list and click **Next**.

Finally, you are given a summary of your settings for the new site. The important things at this stage are what we have called the website – in this case BigDrinks_site – and where we have saved the local root folder – your location will be different to the one shown here.

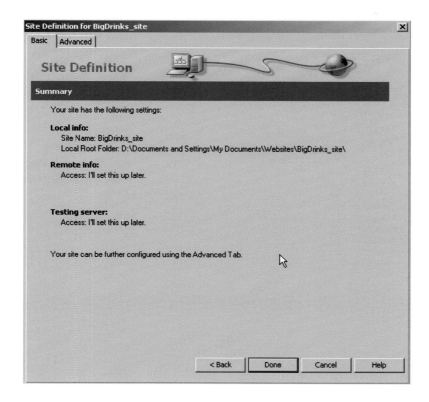

Figure 1.8

 10 Click **Done**.

The Site Definition wizard closes and the welcome screen is revealed.

We've now set up the folder into which we're going to save all our files so we can get on with the next stage, which is planning the website.

STEP 2: PLANNING THE WEBSITE

We need to spend some time planning our website, so first of all we need to think about what will be needed for the site. The whole website at the moment is planned to have three pages. The home page is planned in more detail in Figure 1.9.

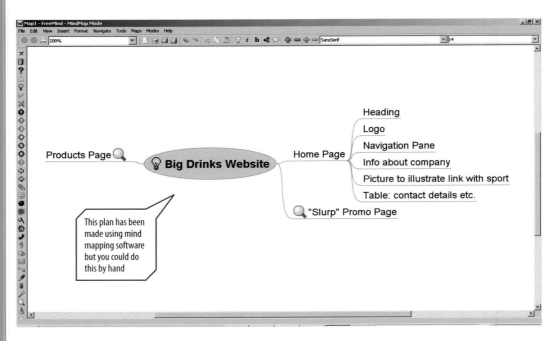

Figure 1.9

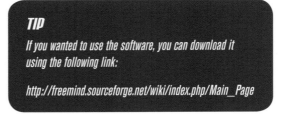

TIP

If you wanted to use the software, you can download it using the following link:

http://freemind.sourceforge.net/wiki/index.php/Main_Page

Now we know what the home page will have to display, we can start the first stage of the design for the page, which is the layout. You could use the table with the drawings that you completed in the 'Get ahead' section in the Introduction.

Figure 1.10 shows a suggested layout for the home page for Big Drinks – yours might be different.

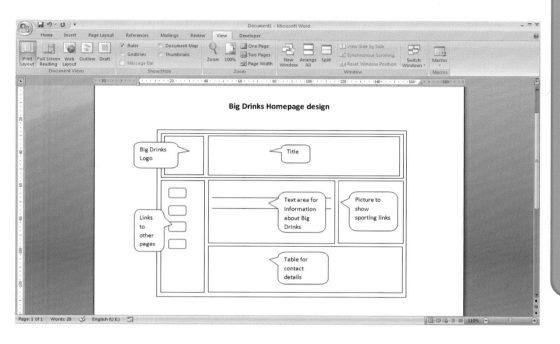

Figure 1.10

Compare your version of the home page with the one shown here and decide on a final layout. We're going to start making each of these sections – like the logo, title and links – into a different frame in the next step. You'll learn more about frames as you read on.

FUNCTIONAL SKILLS

Choosing the right layout – it is important to think about layout because as well as considering who your audience is and whether your document is suitable for them, there are sometimes rules that certain types of documents follow about where to place information in them. These rules are useful because people can more easily identify the information they need if it is always in a similar place. For our website, we have chosen to include a heading banner at the top of the page with the navigation buttons on the left, and up to two columns of information in the rest of the space, which is a standard layout you would see on many websites

STEP 3: USING DREAMWEAVER

Finding your way around

You should have the welcome page displayed on the screen.

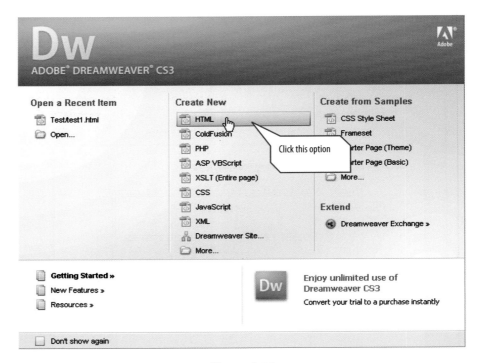

Figure 1.11

 Click the **HTML** button.

The main screen in design view appears:

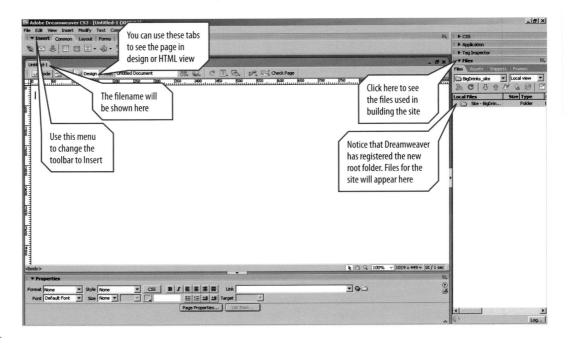

Figure 1.12

12 Let's give the file a name – click **File** and select **Save As**.

 13 Save the file as '**big_drinks_homepage**'.

Frames

Remember we said we were going to create the sections on our page as different frames? Well, frames are simply a way of dividing up a web page so that each section of the page, or frame, can work independently from the others. For example, one frame can be fixed in position and used for navigation buttons whereas another can scroll to reveal the text and pictures in a long document. It makes developing a web page easier because you can make changes to sections without affecting the whole page.

 14 Swap to the **Layout** tab on the **Insert** toolbar.

 15 Click on the **Frames** icon.

 16 Select (click) the **Top Frame** option from the drop-down list:

Left Frame
Right Frame
Top Frame
Bottom Frame
Bottom and Nested Left Frame
Bottom and Nested Right Frame
Left and Nested Bottom Frame
Right and Nested Bottom Frame
Top and Bottom Frames
Left and Nested Top Frames
Right and Nested Top Frame
Top and Nested Left Frames
Top and Nested Right Frame

Figure 1.13

 17 Select **topFrame** from the drop-down menu in the dialogue box, then rename the frame as '**headingFrame**' and click **OK**.

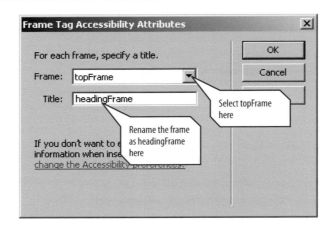

Figure 1.14

Notice that the design window has now created a separate area at the top of the screen – this is where we are eventually going to place the heading.

 If you click in the new heading frame your screen should look like this.

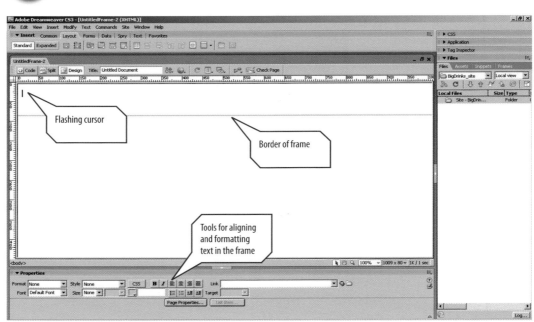

Figure 1.15

19 Before we insert the heading, though, let's create some more frames. In the same way, make a left frame – this will eventually contain the Big Drinks logo. Put your cursor in the heading frame before you create the left frame so that it creates a small frame for the logo within the heading frame. Name the frame '**logoFrame**'.

 20 Make sure the frame is in line with the bottom of the heading frame.

 21 Put your cursor in the main frame and make another frame. Rename this frame '**navFrame**'. Resize the frame so that it is on the left and beneath the logo frame.

The layout should look like this:

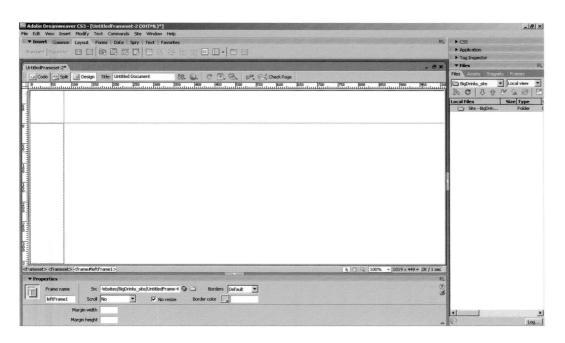

Figure 1.16

 22 Click in the heading frame.

 23 Type in 'Big Drinks Ltd'.

 24 Highlight the text and in **Properties** change the **Format** to **Heading 1** and the **Font** to **Geneva, Arial, Helvetica, sans-serif** and centre the text.

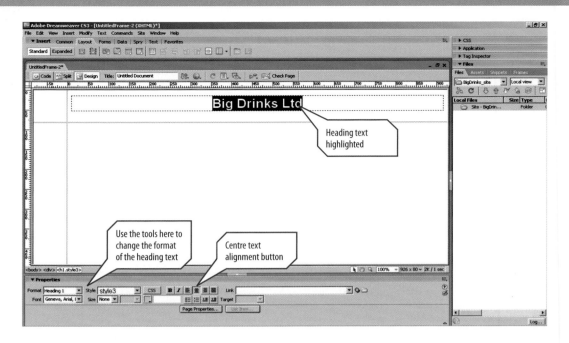

Figure 1.17

The next job is to import the logo for Big Drinks. Remember that Dreamweaver will only manage files for you if they are in the root folder, so we need to copy the logo file into the root folder.

Any website is going to contain many images, so it makes sense to keep the images in their own folder – so let's set that up first.

 Right click on the icon of the site root folder in the **Files** panel.

Figure 1.18

26 Click on **New Folder** in the drop-down menu.

27 Name the new folder 'Images'.

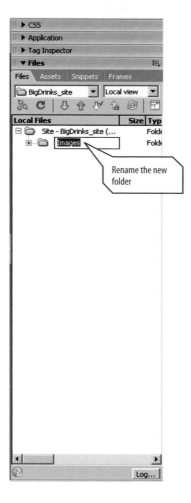

Figure 1.19

28 Right click on the Images folder and select **Explore**.

29 Use the dialogue box to navigate to where the images for the website have been saved on your computer.

Highlight the images listed below and then right click and choose **Copy** from the menu.

big_drinks_logo1

big_drinks_logo2

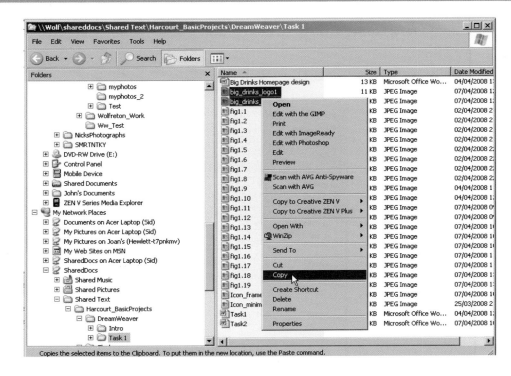

Figure 1.20

 Find your root folder for the website again and right click on the **Images** folder. Choose **Paste** from the menu and you should see your image files appear. Or you can drag the images into the correct folder.

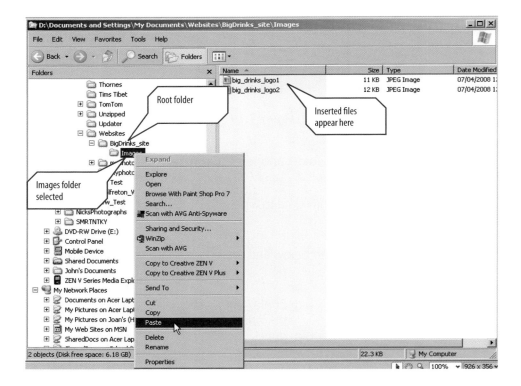

Figure 1.21

Close the dialogue box by clicking on the cross in the top-right corner.

 Back in Dreamweaver, click the **+** next to the name of the **Images** folder in the **Files** pane. You should see your image files listed there.

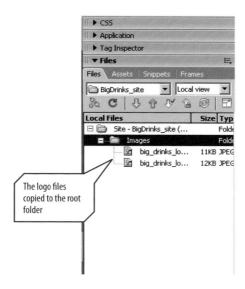

Figure 1.22

Before you can insert the new logo image into the page, however, you first need to save the frame files you have just created. There will be four files to save:

❯ A **big_drinks_frameset** file, which is the file for dividing up the window.

❯ A **headingFrame** file.

❯ A **logoFrame** file.

❯ A **navFrame** file.

 Click **File** and select **Save All**.

 Type '**big_drinks_frameset**' in the **File name** box and click **Save**. Now type in the next filename in the list and click **Save**. Do this until you have saved all four files listed in bold.

Now you can choose one of the two big_drinks_logo images and drag it over to its position to the left of the heading. As you do so, the **Image Tag Accessibility Attributes** dialogue box appears again. Type '**big_drinks_logo1**' (or '**big_drinks_logo2**') into the **Alternate text** box.

SOFTWARE SKILLS
Saving files used in a website

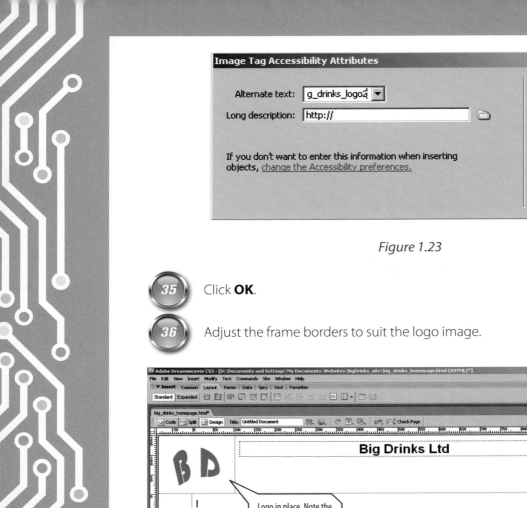

Figure 1.23

35 Click **OK**.

36 Adjust the frame borders to suit the logo image.

Figure 1.24

Testing

Before we go any further, let's check that the site works correctly. You need to check the answers to these questions:

➤ If you close the site, will it open again?

➤ Is the site visible in an Internet browser?

37 Click the cross on the right of the design view window.

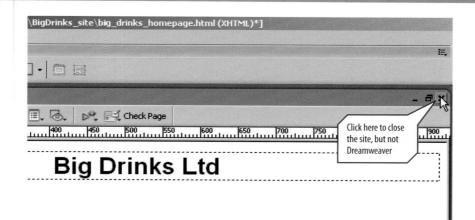

Figure 1.25

FUNCTIONAL SKILLS

Reviewing work – checking your work after each stage is important so that you can identify and fix any problems before you move onto the next stage. If you get to the end of the web build and then find you have a problem – where do you start to look to fix it?

 38 You will be prompted to save the changes you have made to the file big_drinks_homepage and the frame sizes.

The site closes and you are now back to the Dreamweaver welcome screen.

To test if the site opens looking like it did when we closed it, we need to open the frameset file because this contains the instructions for where the frames are placed in the screen.

 39 Open the frameset as shown in Figure 1.26.

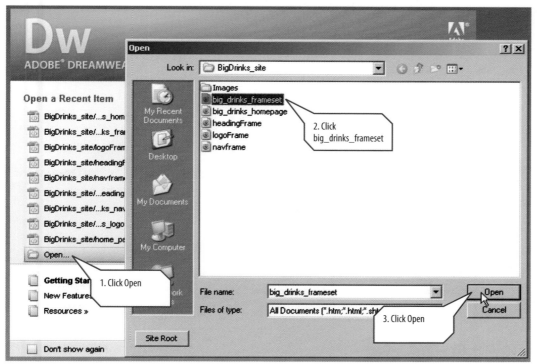

Figure 1.26

Disaster! Where have all the frames gone?

Don't worry, the borders to the frames are transparent and we just need Dreamweaver to show us where they are again.

 Click **View** on the menu bar.

 Select **Visual Aids** and then **Frame Borders** in the sub-menu.

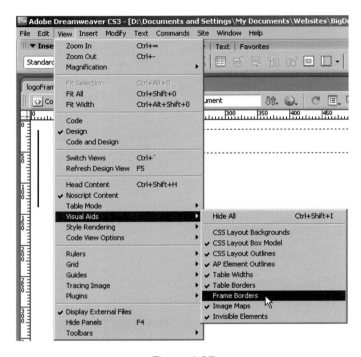

Figure 1.27

Relief!

So on to the next test, to see if it's visible in an Internet browser (this is important to keep checking because it shows you how your page will look when you publish it on the Internet):

 You can *either* click the **Preview/Debug in browser** button on the **Document** toolbar and select the browser that you use for looking at web pages (in Figure 1.28 I have selected Firefox); *or* press **F12**.

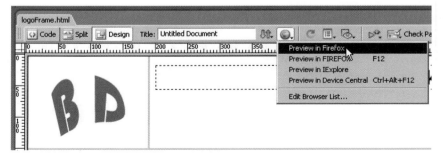

Figure 1.28

And here is the view of the page in my browser:

Figure 1.29

Well, it's not the most impressive web page, but at least we have shown that it works!

Inserting text

So who are Big Drinks Ltd? Let's add some text so that people can find out more about them. We going to import the information (because it's already written) in a file called big_drinks_history.

 Follow the same procedure that we used for the logos (see page 28), create a folder called '**Text**' and copy the big_drinks_history file into the folder.

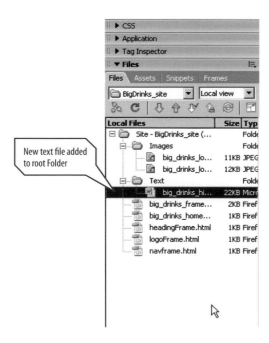

Figure 1.30

45 Drag the file into the bottom-right area of the web page.

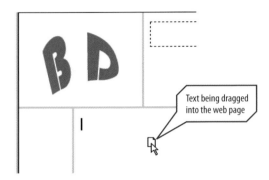

Figure 1.31

The **Insert Document** dialogue box loads.

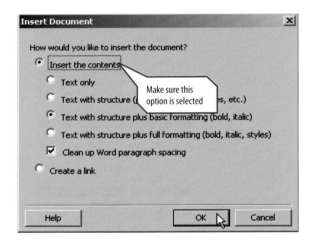

Figure 1.32

46 Make sure that the **Insert the contents** radio button is clicked.

47 Click **OK**.

Your text should now appear.

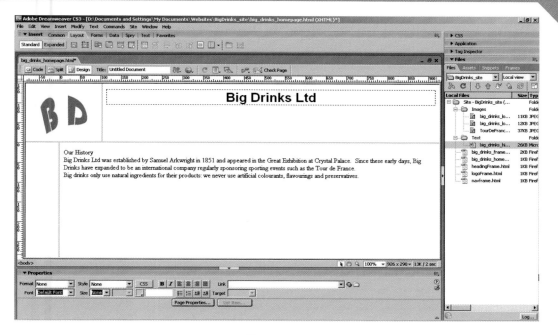

Figure 1.33

 Press **Enter** on the keyboard to move the cursor to the line below the text.

We will leave the formatting of the text until after we have inserted the image that goes in this frame along with the text.

Importing an image

Big Drinks Ltd want to advertise their link with sports events, so we're going to import an image of the Tour de France cycling event, which you will find in a file called Tour_de_France_1.

We chose this image from several that the company supplied because it matches the company's links with international sporting events. The image has been supplied to us so we don't need to worry about budget or copyright as the client has given us permission to use their image. If you don't own the image, you'll need to contact the owner (copyright holder) to get permission to use it.

 Follow the same procedure that we used for the logos to copy the file Tour_de_France_1 to the Images folder.

 Drag the file into the frame that contains the paragraph of text.

The following dialogue box loads:

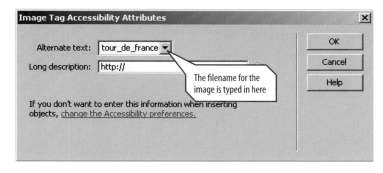

Figure 1.34

SOFTWARE SKILLS
Inserting an image

FUNCTIONAL SKILLS

Selecting suitable images – we have to consider these things when selecting images:

- our client's requirements

- the audience

- the file size (this is important if you want to use the image electronically because large files take a long time to open)

- the amount of money we have to spend on the images (the budget)

- copyright

51 Enter the name of the file as '**Tour_de_France_1**' in the **Alternate text** box.

52 Click **OK**.

The image appears in the design view, but remember to check that the browser can also see the image.

53 Click the **Preview/Debug in browser** button or click **F12**.

Figure 1.35

That's OK, but we want the image on the right of the screen.

54 Close the browser by clicking on the cross to return to Dreamweaver.

55 In Dreamweaver, click on the image.

56 Look at the **Properties** pane at the bottom of the page:

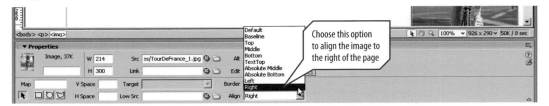

Figure 1.36

57 Open the drop-down list in the **Align** box and choose **Right**.

58 Check again in your browser.

Well, it looks better, but if you check with the original design in Figure 1.10 on page 23, the text and the image appear side by side. We can do this by placing the text and the image in their own boxes and then arranging them next to each other.

Click this icon 📋 on the **Layout** toolbar. Its correct name is an AP element (accurately positioned element) and it draws what looks like a text box.

The cursor changes to a cross. ✛

59 Use this cross to draw a rectangular box about the size of the image.

60 Drag the image into the box.

61 Resize the box to fit the image.

62 Drag the image to the right of the screen in line with the top of the frame.

63 Now make another box to contain the text.

64 Arrange the text and image as in Figure 1.37:

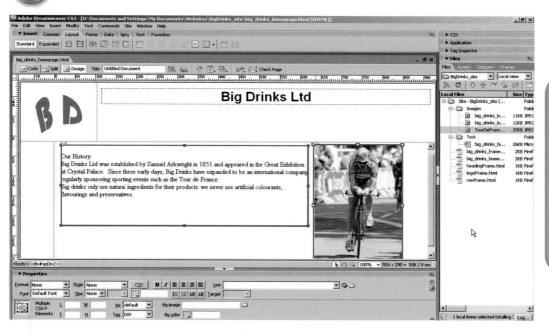

Figure 1.37

TIP

Try to get into the habit of always checking your work as it will appear on the web (browser) after each new element that you add.

65 We've added something new to our page so let's look at the result in your browser.

Big Drinks Ltd

Our History

Big Drinks Ltd was established by Samuel Arkwright in 1851 and appeared in the Great Exhibition at Crystal Palace. Since these early days, Big Drinks have expanded to be an international company regularly sponsoring sporting events such as the Tour de France.

Big drinks only use natural ingredients for their products: we never use artificial colourants, flavourings and preservatives.

Figure 1.38

Does your page look like this?

Inserting tables

The final job is to insert a table to contain the contact details of Big Drinks Ltd – their postal address, website URL and email address.

66 Draw another box below the text already on-screen and make it the same width.

67 Click inside the box.

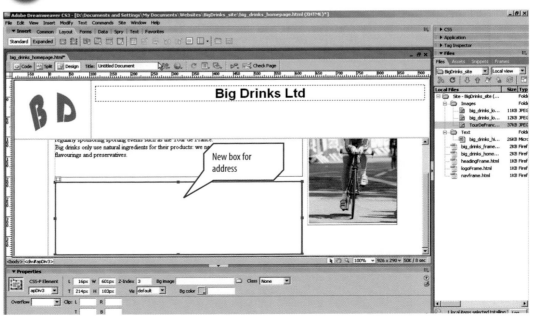

Figure 1.39

Click the **Table** button on either the **Common** or the **Layout** toolbars.

The Table dialogue box opens:

Figure 1.40

 Make the settings as in Figure 1.40 and click **OK**. The caption is the heading that will appear in your table.

A small version of the table appears on-screen, which you can resize to fill the width of the box you have drawn.

Use the handles to resize the table:

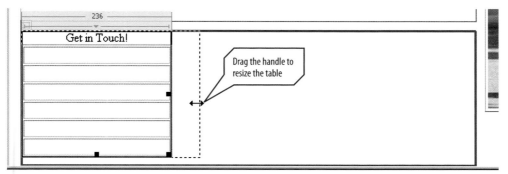

Figure 1.41

71 Type the contact details shown below into the table.

Big Drinks Ltd
Thirsty Works
THIRSK
YO50 1AA
Website: bigdrinksltd.co.uk
email: thirst@bigdrinksltd.co.uk

Big Drinks Ltd

Our History
Big Drinks Ltd was established by Samuel Arkwright in 1851 and appeared in the Great Exhibition at Crystal Palace. Since these early days, Big Drinks have expanded to be an international company regularly sponsoring sporting events such as the Tour de France.
Big drinks only use natural ingredients for their products: we never use artificial colourants, flavourings and preservatives.

Get in Touch!

| Big Drinks Ltd |
| Thirsty Works |
| THIRSK |
| YO 50 1AA |
| Website: bigdrinksltd.co.uk |
| email: thirst@bigdrinksltd.co.uk |

Figure 1.42

 72 Check that the table appears correctly in the browser.

73 Click **Save All**.

74 Close Dreamweaver.

That's it!

Of course there is a lot more formatting we can do to improve the look of the website now that we have the layout, but we will leave that for the next Task.

GET AHEAD

To prepare for the next Task try to complete this table (you will need to redraw and enlarge it to accommodate the drawings):

Problem with the website	Your proposed solution	What it will look like (insert a drawing)
No page for catalogue of products		
No page for Slurp		
Difficult to read fonts		
No background		
No links		

CHECKPOINT

Check that you know how to:

> Create a root folder.

> Work methodically and add asset files and folders to the root folder.

> Create and resize frames.

> Rename and copy files and folders.

> Save the files that are used in a website. In particular understand the purpose of each of the files.

> Thoroughly test a website.

> View a page in a web browser.

> Add a text file and its text to the website.

> Add an image file and the image to the website.

> Use AP elements to contain text, an image and a table.

> Add a table to a website.

ASSESSMENT POINT

Now let's assess the work. Look back at the table at the beginning of this section (**Target point**) and decide on which of the statements you can answer 'Yes' to.

Did you do as well as you expected? Could you improve your work? Use Word to write a comment to show what you could do to improve your work and remember this when starting your next ICT project.

TASK BRIEF

Big Drinks are happy with the planning you have done for the website and now want you to take the design further.

BRIEF

To recap… Big Drinks Ltd is a manufacturer of soft drinks, including their most recent drink, 'Slurp'. The website will be used by shops and other businesses to view and order Big Drinks' products to sell in their own stores.

Big Drinks require you to:

> Add the Products Page and Slurp Page.

> Link the pages together.

> Include buttons to use to navigate between the pages.

> Create a colour scheme for the site.

> Include information about the product Slurp.

SOFTWARE SKILLS

You will learn how to:

- Add new files to your website
- Add new pages to your website and link them using hyperlinks
- Incorporate 'rollover' buttons
- Use the Property Inspector to change the formatting of frames, backgrounds and fonts
- Use form controls
- Add movie files to a website

FUNCTIONAL SKILLS

As you work through this task the Functional Skills tabs will explain to you why the decisions have been made to respond to the brief in the way shown in Task 2 and explain why you would choose to:

- Organise the files in your website
- Select appropriate images
- Format your web pages to improve their design and appeal
- Test your website as it is developed to locate any errors

CAPABILITY

You will be demonstrating your capability in matching your choice of font and audio to your audience if you complete the Get Ahead section.

VOCABULARY

You should learn these new words and understand what they mean:

- Property
- Colour picker
- Flash
- Rollover
- Hyperlink

RESOURCES

You need to open the website you began building in Task 1 and download the image slurp_image1.jpg. There is a version of this site available to download if your website didn't work out. Click on the file big_drinks_frameset.html to open the site. You should download the Big Drinks site folder and image from www.payne-gallway.co.uk

TARGET POINT

Turn the page to see your Target Points for this task.

TARGET POINT

Have a look at the following statements before you start your task so you know what you are aiming for.

Although you will not make your own decisions on the design of the form in Task 2, you can use what you learn here to help with other work that will be awarded a particular level.

Level 3	Level 4	Level 5	Level 6
You have followed the instructions to set up new files	You have successfully set up a new file	You have shown that new files have been incorporated into your website	
You have added a button to your website	You have configured a button to change the page loaded in a web browser	You have tested a hyperlink to check its function	
You have used formatting tools such as those used to change background colour or fonts	You have used tools in the Property Inspector to change background colours to match those in the advert image	You have recognised the need to use colours that relate to a product	
You have used navigation tools to locate the image file	You have loaded the image file into the heading frame	You have used the Files panel to move the image file to the Images folder in the website root folder	You recognise the importance of order when arranging files in a website
You have, with help if needed, located a movie file using navigation techniques	You have inserted a movie in the Slurp web page	You have inserted the movie in the correct part of the web page, checked that it works correctly and saved the file to the root folder	You have saved your movie file to a separate folder within the root folder
You have recognised and used the controls on the form	You have altered the properties of a control using the Property Inspector	You have checked that the controls function correctly	You have checked that the form and its controls function correctly in more than one web browser
You have used a web browser to view your site	You have tested your site using a web browser and put right any errors	You have regularly tested your website to locate and put right errors	You have used more than one browser to test your website, recognising that users of the site may have different browsers
You have saved your work	You have saved files using appropriate filenames		

BEFORE WE START

Task 1 was focused on developing a plan for the Big Drinks website and the layout for its home page. During Task 2 you will take the development of the Big Drinks website forward by adding further pages, linking them together and making the site more attractive.

ASSETS AND OPENING DREAMWEAVER

Before you start, make sure that you have completed the activities from Task 1. There is one extra asset needed for this task, but you will not need to download this until later, so just:

 Load Dreamweaver.

 Follow the instructions in Figure 2.1 to select the site that you made in Task 1.

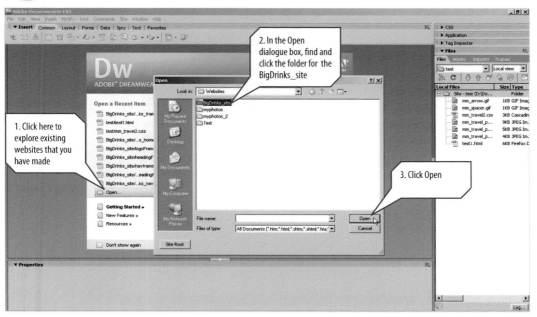

Figure 2.1

 Follow the instructions in Figure 2.2 to open the file.

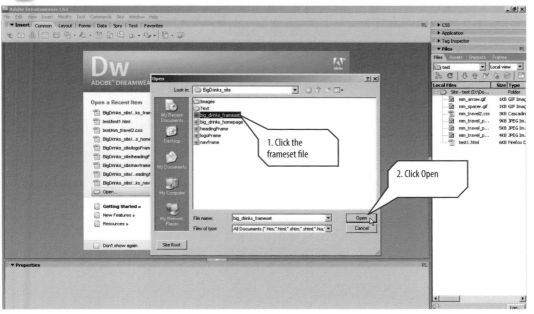

Figure 2.2

ADDING TWO MORE PAGES

Each page is a file, so we will have to make two more files.

First of all, look at the **Files** panel on the right of the screen; it may not show the files for your Big Drinks site:

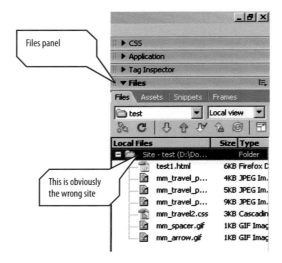

Figure 2.3

 Click the button to the right of the title to the **Files** panel (see Figure 2.4).

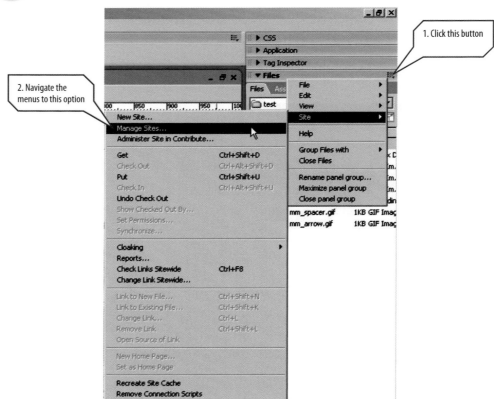

Figure 2.4

You should see the following dialogue box. Follow the instructions to complete your selection.

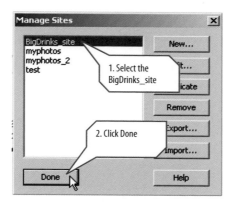

Figure 2.5

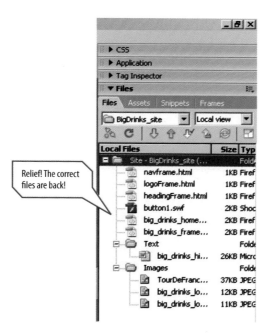

Figure 2.6

Now to insert the two new pages: for these we are going to use sample pages. These are partly completed already, so this should save us some work.

FUNCTIONAL SKILLS

Using templates – using the right template can speed up the process of creating your page and can help to remind you of the type of information you should include. Here we have chosen a template called Product Catalog because we want to create a page that displays the products Big Drinks sell

⑤ Click on **File** on the menu bar and the select **New** from the drop-down menu:

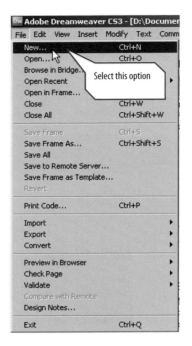

Figure 2.7

Follow the instructions in Figure 2.8 to select your sample page. Make sure all of your settings are the same as those shown here.

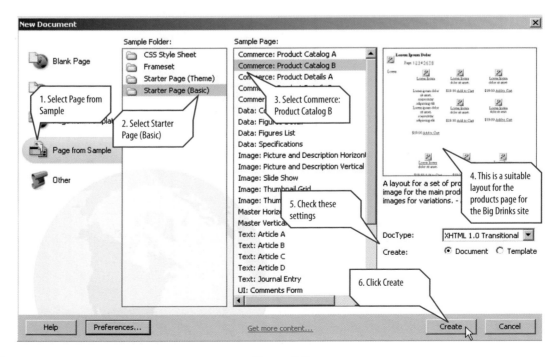

Figure 2.8

The new page loads into the Dreamweaver design screen:

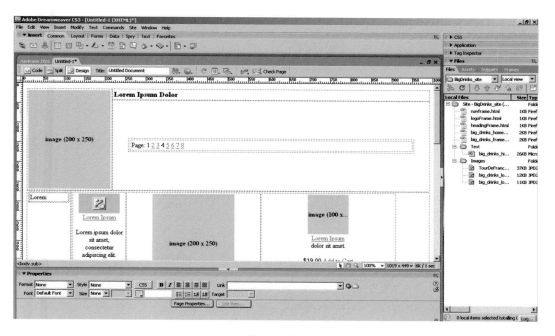

Figure 2.9

You need to save the page before we do anything else, so let's do that next:

6   Click on **File** in the menu bar and then select **Save As**.

7   Call the file '**big_drinks_productspage**' and then save it.

SOFTWARE SKILLS
Saving new files to the root folder

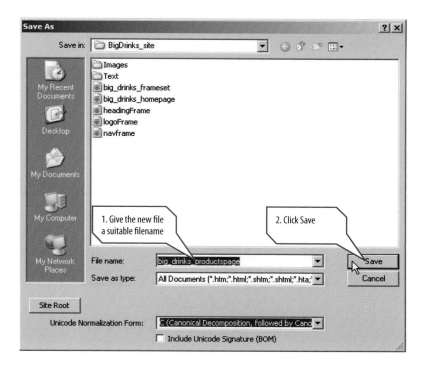

Figure 2.10

When you have saved the file, just check that you can see that it has been added to the files in the **Files** panel:

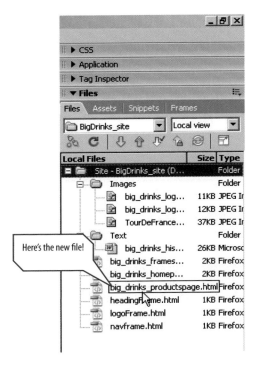

Figure 2.11

We said we were adding two new pages so you need to add another page, which will be used to advertise Slurp. Go back to the **New Document** dialogue box (**File** > **New**).

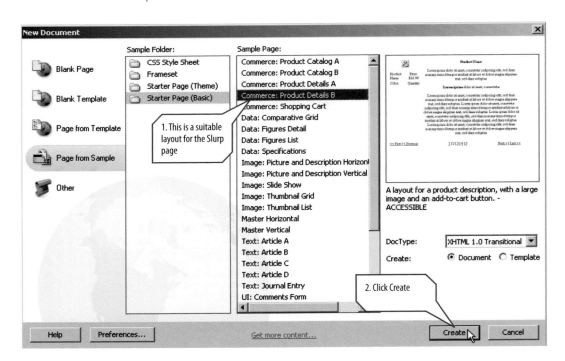

Figure 2.12

Select **Commerce: Product Details B** as shown in Figure 2.12 and then click **Create**.

 Now save the file as you did with the products page. This time call the file:

big_drinks_slurppage

 Look at the **Files** panel to check that the new file has been added to the website.

FORMATTING THE HOME PAGE

The first thing for us to do is to tidy the layout that you made during Task 1.

Make sure you have the home page showing on screen. You can do this by clicking the home page file on the **Files** panel.

You probably can't see the edges of the frames, so make these visible as you did in Task 1 (**View** > **Visual Aids** > **Frame Borders**).

The vertical left-hand border is to be used for links to other pages and will probably need to be wider. If we place a button in the frame, then we can see exactly how wide the frame needs to be.

 Click in the left-hand vertical frame beneath the 'BD' logo.

 Click the **Flash Button** icon in the **Common** tab of the toolbar (if your copy of Dreamweaver doesn't show the Flash Button icon, read the next tip).

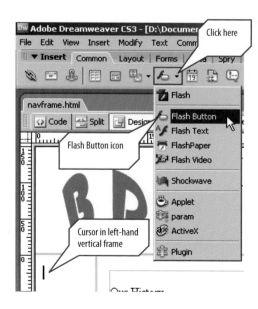

Figure 2.13

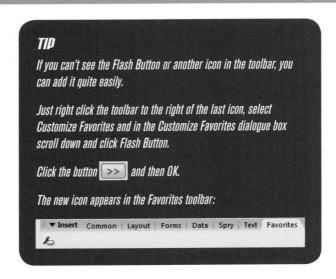

TIP

If you can't see the Flash Button or another icon in the toolbar, you can add it quite easily.

Just right click the toolbar to the right of the last icon, select Customize Favorites and in the Customize Favorites dialogue box scroll down and click Flash Button.

Click the button >> *and then OK.*

The new icon appears in the Favorites toolbar:

You will see the following dialogue box.

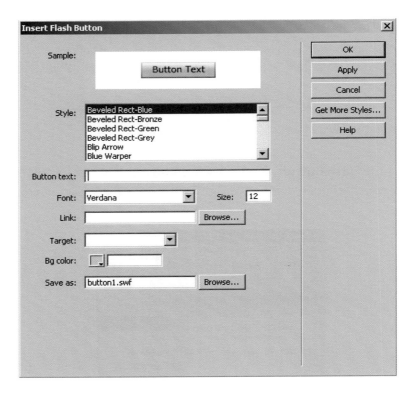

Figure 2.14

 In the **Style** box, select the **Diamond Spinner**. This style makes your button change as you roll over it. We'll see how it works later on.

 Type '**Products**' into the **Button Text** box.

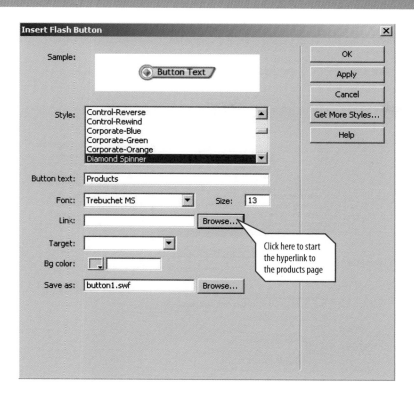

Figure 2.15

We want the button to form a link (this is called a 'hyperlink') to the products page in the website, so:

 Next to the **Link** box, click on the **Browse** button.

The **Select file** dialogue box loads:

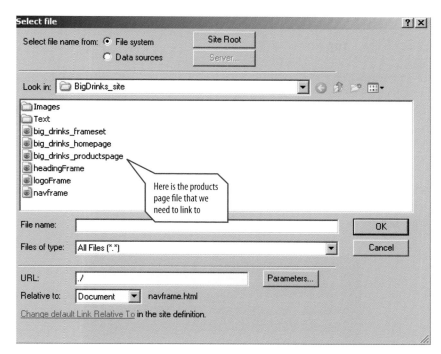

Figure 2.16

15 Click on the products page file (big_drinks_productspage) and then click **OK**.

You are returned to the **Insert Flash Button** dialogue box.

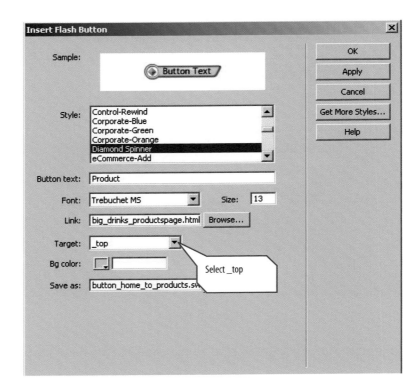

Figure 2.17

16 Click the drop-down box next to **Target**.

17 Select (click) **_top** from the list.

This ensures that the hyperlink goes to the top of the products page.

18 Rename the button (it is probably named something like 'button1.swf' at the moment). Give the button a filename that relates to its action, like:

button_home_to_products.swf

and type it into the **Save As** section.

19 Click **OK**.

> **TIP**
> It's important that you are specific with your button names because you could end up with a lot of buttons and you need to be able to identify which is which easily.

20 The **Flash Accessibility Attributes** dialogue box loads:

The text that you add here can be used by programs that are designed to help people with poor eyesight, often by reading out the text for them. The **Access key** and **Tab index** boxes can be left blank.

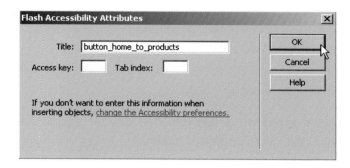

Figure 2.18

21 Type in a suitable title (it makes sense to use the name of the button's file as shown in Figure 2.17).

22 Click **OK**.

Notice that the new file shows in the **Files** panel:

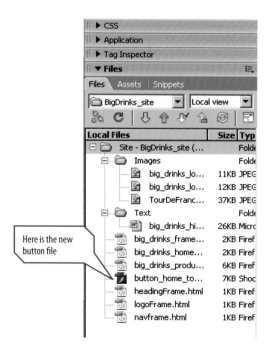

Figure 2.19

You've created the link for the button so that it will take you to another page of your website, but does the button actually work and link you to the right page? Let's find out how to check.

 Click the **Preview/Debug in browser** button on the **Document** bar (check on Figure intro.4 in the Introduction if you can't recall where this is). Or press **F12** on your keyboard.

 Select (click) the browser that you use for the Internet.

 Click **OK** on the save warning dialogue box.

The home page loads in the browser. Now you can click on the products button and check that it loads the products page.

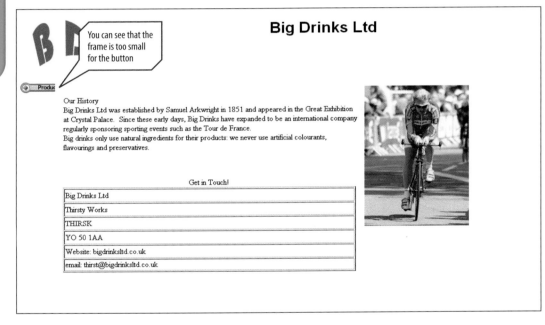

Figure 2.20

Look at the effect of the spinning diamond when you hover the mouse pointer over the button! This is called a 'rollover' because the activity of the object changes as you 'roll over' it with your mouse; we will use the idea again in Task 3.

There are some less attractive features though. For example, the frame seems to mask some of the button and the only way to move to the home page from the products page is by using the back button on the browser.

Let's solve the frame problem first.

Close the browser to return to the Dreamweaver screen.

If you can't see the borders follow these instructions.

 Click **View** on the menu bar and select **Visual Aids** from the drop-down list.

28 In the sub-list click **Frame Borders**.

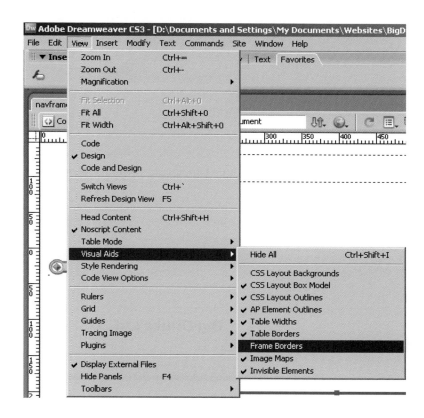

Figure 2.21

Now that you can see the frame borders it is easy to click and drag the lines at the edges of the border to resize them so that they're large enough to view the whole of the button.

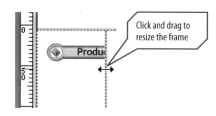

Figure 2.22

While we are thinking about the frames, why not make the borders of the heading frame and the navigation frame (the buttons column) visible in the browser? Let's do that next:

29 Click on the border to the navframe so that it is highlighted and set the **Property Inspector** as shown in Figure 2.23.

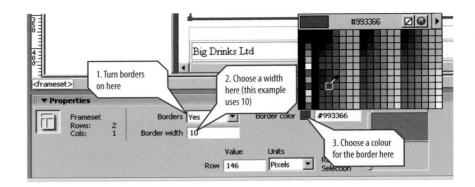

Figure 2.23

30 Once you have made the settings for the border, check that it works by loading the site into your browser as you did previously, using the **Preview/Debug** option.

31 It looks good to have a heading frame border, so click on the border and set it in the same way.

Look at the result in the browser and check that it is suitable.

Figure 2.24

It works as we expected it to, but a different background to the white screen would be a good idea as the screen looks quite bland at the moment. We should use the colours associated with Big Drinks for this, so let's check the colours that are used in the advert for the product 'Slurp'.

The blue and green are colours associated with Slurp and Big Drinks so we should use these colours in the website

Figure 2.25

 Click in the heading frame so that the cursor is located within this frame, as this is where we eventually want the picture of the Slurp advert to appear.

 Click the **Common** tab on the **Insert** toolbar.

 Click the image icon.

The **Select Image Source** dialogue box loads. Choose the image that you downloaded at the start from the location that you saved it in:

slurp_image1.jpg

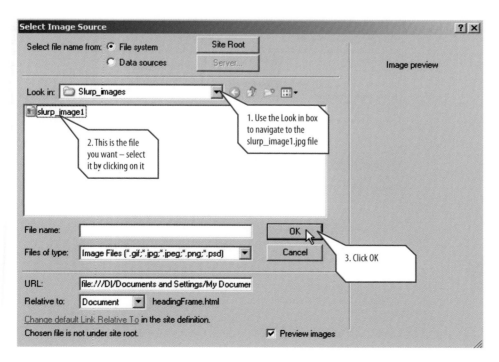

Figure 2.26

35 Navigate to the file and select it as shown in Figure 2.26.

A warning arrives:

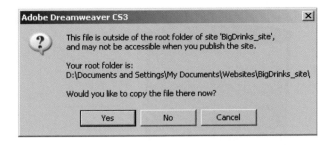

Figure 2.27

> **TIP**
>
> Remember how we said it's important to organise your files for a website? Well, this message shows you why – any file that isn't in your root folder will not be recognised when you launch your site onto the browser and your website will not work as you intended it to.

36 Click **Yes** because later on we will need the picture for the Slurp page of the website.

The **Copy File As** dialogue box opens:

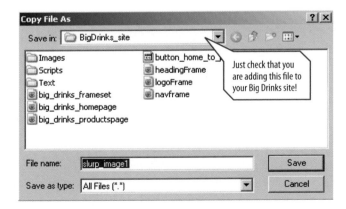

Figure 2.28

37 Click **Save**.

38 Type the name

> slurp_image1

into the **Alternate text** box in the **Image Tag Accessibility Attributes** dialogue box and click **OK**.

You will notice that part of the Slurp advert image appears in the heading frame:

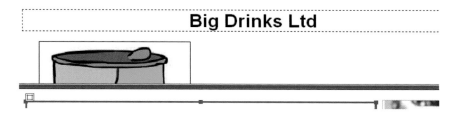

Figure 2.29

 39 Click in the left-hand vertical frame (the 'navframe') so that the text cursor flashes in the frame.

In the **Property Inspector** there is a button marked **Page Properties**. [Page Properties...]

40 Click the button!

The **Page Properties** dialogue box loads. The mouse pointer changes to the **Color Picker**, which allows you to pick a colour.

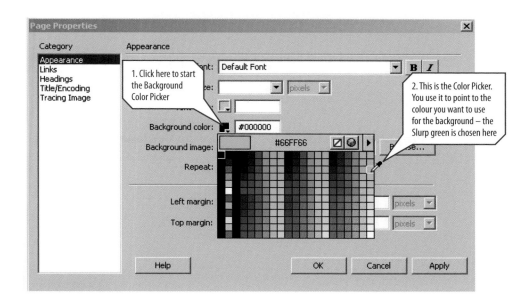

Figure 2.30

If you place the picker over the green part of the Slurp can that you have placed in the header frame and click, this will set the colour for the background of the navframe to exactly the same colour as that used on the can. Magic!

 Click **OK**.

Now click on the Flash button that says Products and change the background colour to the same green.

 Do the same for the heading and logo frames, but use the blue colour on the Slurp can for these frames.

You don't need the slurp_image1 in the heading frame – we just used it to pick our colours – so:

 Click on the image of the can and press the **Delete** key on the keyboard.

You could also change the colour of the main frame.

As well as the background colours we should style our font to one that is suitable.

> **TIP**
> When selecting font styles you always need to consider if it's easy to read on screen as well as whether it's a font that all computers will be able to recognise. It's better that your website displays as you meant it to look than if you choose a wacky font that might not be available on some computers. Using a standard font is therefore advisable.

Let's tackle the 'Our History' heading first:

 Highlight 'Our History' by clicking and dragging the cursor across it.

Use the **Property Inspector** to change the font to **Verdana**, size **24, white**.

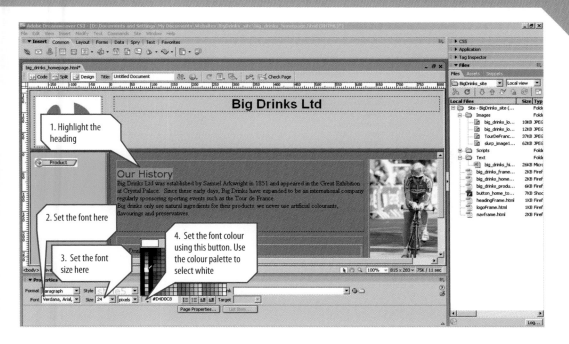

Figure 2.31

 Do the same for the rest of the 'History' text. This time the size should be 16 and the colour the same as the blue of the can. Remember to use the Color Picker for selecting the colour.

 Now format the text in the 'Get in Touch!' table. Click on the table to highlight it and then press **Ctrl** and **a** together to highlight the whole table.

That's all we're going to do on the home page. We haven't done anything with the Slurp page yet, so let's get on with this next.

Slurp is a new product from Big Drinks, so we will see if we can make the page especially attractive for visitors. One way of doing this would be to arrange a video to be played once the page loads, but first of all we need to set up a hyperlink to the page from the home page.

The process of setting up the hyperlink is exactly the same as you have used for the button and hyperlink to the products page. Click on the navframe and then click on the Flash button icon. Refer back to Figures 2.13–2.19 if you need some help. Here are the settings for the **Insert Flash Button** dialogue box:

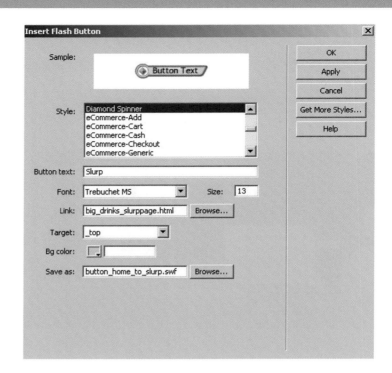

Figure 2.32

Remember to reset the background colour of the button so that it blends in with the green of the Navigation frame:

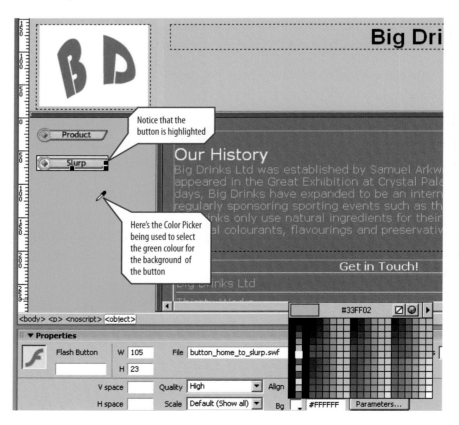

Figure 2.33

Now check that the button 'works' by loading the website into your browser – see Figure 2.20.

 Close the web browser window to return to the main Dreamweaver screen.

 Swap to the Slurp page by double clicking 'big_drinks_slurppage' in the files pane:

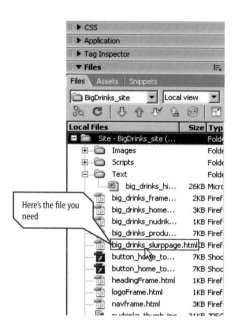

Figure 2.34

The Slurp page looks uninteresting and just has placehoders instead of Slurp pictures and text. Not for long though!

 Click the placeholder titled 'image', at the top left of the screen.

 Swap to the **Common** tab of the **Insert** toolbar and click the **Media arrow** button:

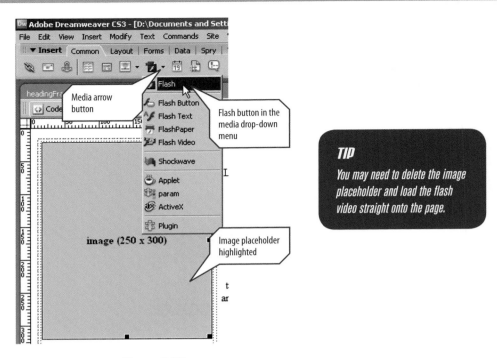

Figure 2.35

TIP

You may need to delete the image placeholder and load the flash video straight onto the page.

52 Click the Flash button in the drop-down menu.

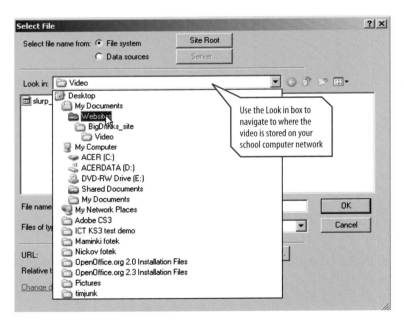

Figure 2.36

53 Use the **Look in** box to navigate to where the Slurp video is stored on your school computer system. You are looking for the file:

Slurp_video.swf

54 Once you have found the file, click on its filename and click **OK**.

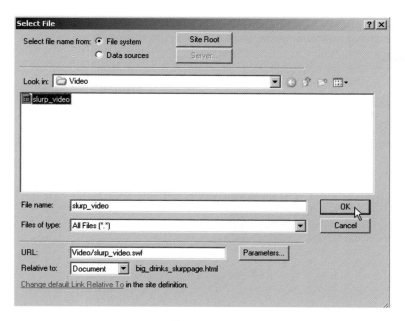

Figure 2.37

 55 A warning appears stating that the file is not in your root folder and asking whether you would like Dreamweaver to copy the video to the root folder. Of course you do, so click **Yes**.

 56 Set up a new folder for the video and name the folder '**Video**'.

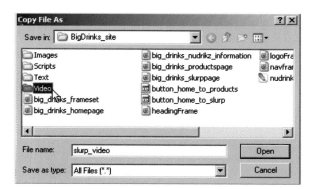

Figure 2.38

 57 Click **Open** and then **Save** so that the copy of the video is stored in the new Video folder.

 58 Give the video the title

slurp_video

in the **Object Tag Accessibility Attributes** dialogue box, and click **OK**.

The page doesn't look much different in Dreamweaver, but will once it is viewed on the web. Let's check this next.

59 Check that the video plays correctly by loading the page into your web browser as we have done previously.

Figure 2.39

That certainly makes for more interest on the Slurp page!

Now let's get on with the rest of the page. This page allows users of the website to make orders for Big Drinks products.

Let's see how we change the information on the page to show what we need. We start with altering one of the controls on the page. Controls are objects that can be changed to suit a particular purpose.

60 Close the web browser and return to the Dreamweaver screen.

61 Scroll down the page until you find the list/menu control:

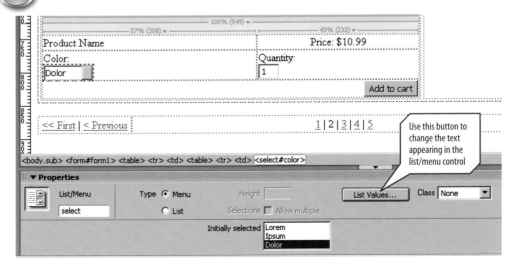

Figure 2.40

Highlight the list/menu control by clicking *in* it; when you have done this correctly, you will notice that the Property Inspector looks like that shown in Figure 2.40.

 Click the **List Values** button.

The List Values dialogue box enables you to change the contents of the control so that your user can select the number of cans of Slurp that they want to order:

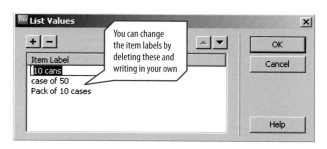

Figure 2.41

 Delete the placeholder text in the **List Values** dialogue box and type in the new text to show the amounts Slurp is sold in:

> 10 cans
> Case of 50
> Pack of 10 cases

 Click **OK**.

The list/menu control will not work on the form until you load it into your web browser. Try that now!

 Now you need to change the title of this drop down list. Highlight Color and change it to:

Slurp is available in packs of:

> 10 cans (£10.99)
> Case of 50 (£50.00)
> Pack of 10 cases (£450.00)

That's all of the controls changed. Now for some more tidying.

 Delete the image placeholder (be careful to highlight it first)!

 Delete the 'Product Name' placeholder text in the right hand column on the page.

Now we need to replace it with the text from the file:

Slurp_information.doc

Click **File** on the menu bar and select **Import** in the drop-down list.

 Click on **Word Document** in the sub-menu:

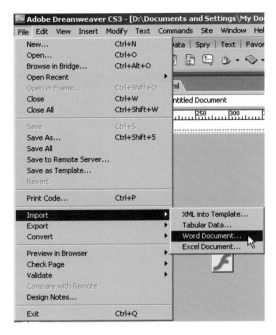

Figure 2.42

 Use the **Import Word Document** dialogue box to navigate to the file slurp_information

 Click on the filename and then click **Open**:

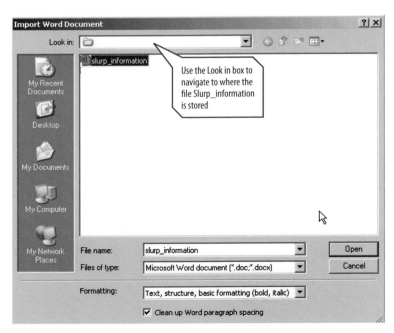

Figure 2.43

The new text appears on the Slurp page.

Place your cursor at the start of the text and press the **Enter** key twice.

 Click at the top of the page again and type in the heading '**Slurp**'.

 Change all of the text to **Geneva**, **Bold**.

 Highlight the heading Slurp and centre the text.

 Change the format to **Heading 1**:

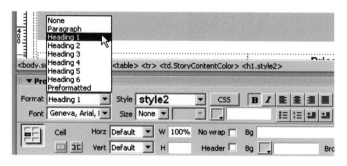

Figure 2.44

 Highlight the Slurp Information text and make it left aligned.

 Insert the image of the Slurp can in the same way as you inserted the Big Drinks logo in Task 1, using the **Images** button on the **Common** tab.

Insert a Flash button and use it to link to the home page. The settings are:

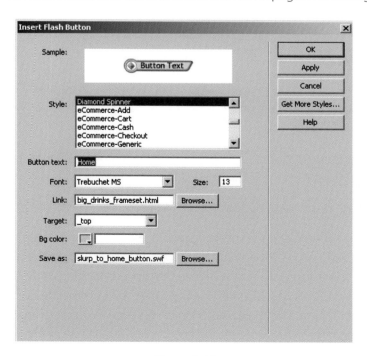

Figure 2.45

81 Finally, use the Big drinks colours to change the background of the Slurp page.

The finished page!

Figure 2.46

 82 Check that the site works by previewing it through your browser as you have done previously.

That's it!

GET AHEAD

There is more you could do to the web page and it would be good practice to work on your own to make sure you have understood and remembered the skills we have just covered. Some ideas to get you started are:

> Change the font used for the title to the Slurp page. You could look for a font which is more like that used on the can.

> Set up a Flash button and hyperlink from the products page to the home page.

> If you have a sound file, or the means to record your voice, you can embed a sound track in the Slurp page. Perhaps you might use the opportunity to describe the product or just play some appropriate music while the movie is running. You need to use the Plugin tool which is found in the Media button on the Common tab of the Insert toolbar. This requires a bit of experimentation because there are many different sound file types and not all web browsers will be able to play all types of file. Good luck!

CHECKPOINT

Check that you know how to:

➤ Open an existing website.

➤ Add more pages to a website and organise the panel display to show files associated with your website.

➤ Use sample pages to reduce the amount of work.

➤ Save new files in your website's root folder.

➤ Add a Flash button.

➤ Add a hyperlink to another page.

➤ Check a web page in a browser.

➤ Resize frames.

➤ Use the Property Inspector to change the look of frames, frame borders, fonts and layout of text.

➤ Import new images into your website.

➤ Use Color Picker to match colours.

➤ Insert a movie file into a web page.

➤ Modify a form by altering the properties of its controls.

ASSESSMENT POINT

Now let's assess the work. Look back at the table at the beginning of this section (**Target point**) and decide on which of the statements you can answer 'Yes' to.

Did you do as well as you expected? Could you improve your work? Use Word to write a comment to show what you could do to improve your work and remember this when starting your next ICT project.

TASK BRIEF

Big Drinks are happy with the way you have put the Slurp page together and want you to complete the design of the site.

BACKGROUND...

Big Drinks Ltd is a manufacturer of soft drinks, including their most recent drink, 'Slurp'. The company require a new website to advertise their business and its products and they're looking for a design company to build it for them. The website will be used by shops and other businesses to view and order Big Drinks' products to sell in their own stores.

Big Drinks require you to:

 Include information about Big Drink's other products that users of the website can access if they want to.

SOFTWARE SKILLS

You will learn how to:

> Add new assets to folders in the website

> Use AP elements to display enlarged images and information

> Use the Property Inspector to change the properties of AP elements

> Use behaviours and events to control the display of AP elements

FUNCTIONAL SKILLS

As you work through this task the Functional Skills tabs will explain to you why the decisions have been made to respond to the brief in the way shown in Task 3 and explain why you would choose to:

> Organise the assets in your website

> Insert assets into AP element frames

> Format your web pages to improve their design and appeal

> Test your website as it is developed to locate any errors

CAPABILITY

You will be demonstrating capability if you complete the Get Ahead section where you will include functions on your webpage suitable for your audience.

VOCABULARY

You should learn these new words and understand what they mean.

> Element (as used in the term 'AP element')

> Behaviour (notice the American spelling used in Dreamweaver: Behavior)

> Event

> Rollover

> Layers

> Pixel

TARGET POINT

Turn the page to see your Target Points for this task.

Level 3	Level 4	Level 5	Level 6
You have used navigation methodically to find asset files	You have copied the asset files to your website	You have copied the asset files into the correct folder (images) in your website	You have shown that you understand the need for copies of all files in the root folder of the website
You have added an AP element to a web page	You have used the Property Inspector to change the size, name and visibility of an AP element	You have linked a behaviour to an AP element	You have successfully linked an event to a behaviour and tested the functioning of the page

BEFORE WE START

The structure of the Big Drinks website is now complete. This task is about adding content and making the site user-friendly.

ASSETS AND OPENING DREAMWEAVER

Before you start, make sure that you have completed the activities from Task 2 and have downloaded and saved the three assets needed for this task, then …

 Load Dreamweaver.

 Select and open the Big Drinks site:

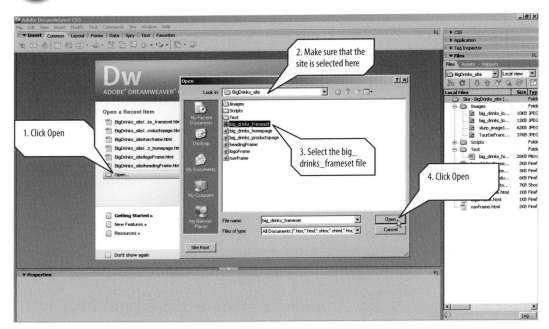

Figure 3.1

Swap to the products page so that it is in your design view. You do this by double clicking the file in the **Files** panel:

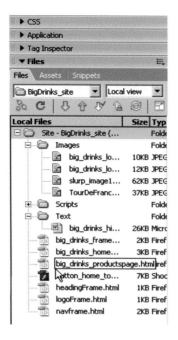

Figure 3.2

The template for this page is another form and is more complicated than we need so let's start by deleting the sections that we don't need. You can reduce the size of the products page by zooming out (**View** > **Zoom Out**) to make it easier to see all of the sections on the page, so that you can see the sections we are going to delete.

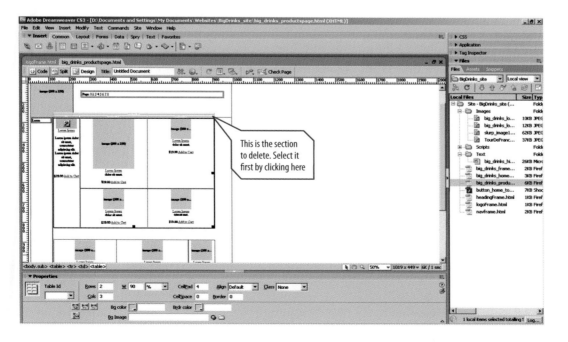

Figure 3.3

4 Figure 3.3 shows the section that we need to delete so select the section by clicking on the edge as shown in the figure.

5 Press **Delete** on your keyboard.

Now we are only left with the sections we can make use of and what looks like a much more manageable layout. Look at Figure 3.4 to show you how we are going to make use of the space on the web page.

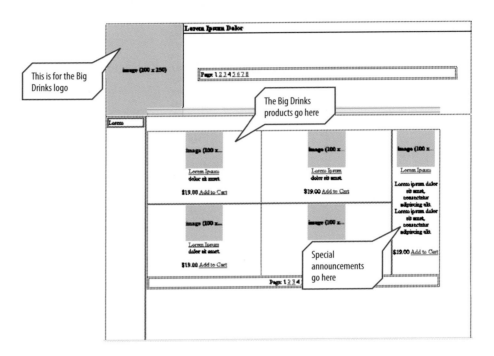

Figure 3.4

The next figure gives you some idea of what you could make your page look like if you formatted your page using the skills you will have learned in Tasks 2 and 3. Task 3 teaches you how to create the highlighted section and the Get Ahead section makes further suggestions about how you could develop your page to look more like the example shown.

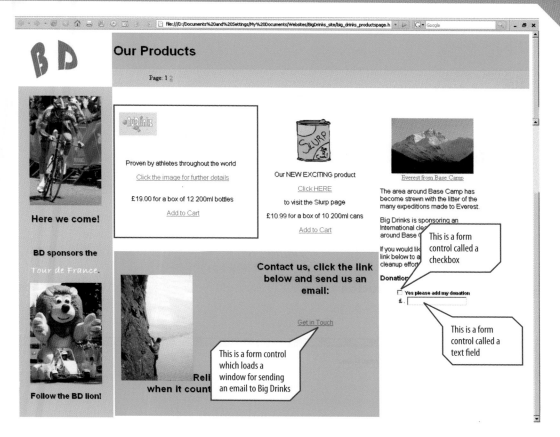

Figure 3.5

6 We can't work on the page at this scale so zoom in again to make the sections larger (**View** > **Zoom In**).

CREATING A ROLLOVER

You will probably have noticed a 'rollover' effect when using the Internet. For instance, often, if you hover over buttons, a box giving you more information pops up – that's a rollover effect. But the effect can take many forms – in this instance we are going to use images and make them enlarge as you roll over a thumbnail image. Many online clothing and sports equipment shops use this method to display their catalogue so that you can see the clothes you're interested in buying in more detail when enlarged.

You are going to set up this rollover effect for items on the products page. To do this you need two versions of the same image – a small version which will be the 'thumbnail' and a larger version used for the rollover.

To create this effect each picture has to be held inside the special frame called an AP element, which we came across in Task 1. The AP element frames act as layers in the web page where only the top layer is ever visible, just like a deck of cards – there are 52 cards in the pile, and you can change which card is at the top but you can only ever see the top card.

By moving the layers up and down we can control when the thumbnail and the large image are visible.

This is how to do it:

Click the **Layout** tab on the **Insert** toolbar.

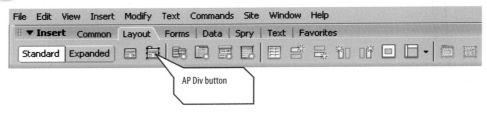

Figure 3.6

Click the **AP Div button** and draw a rectangle (your AP element) near to the first item in the products page:

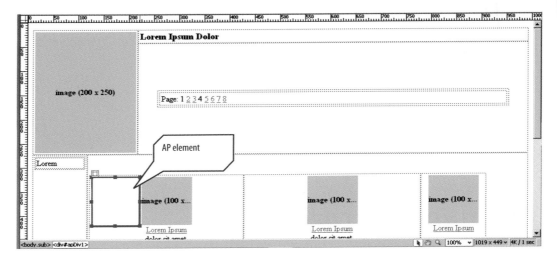

Figure 3.7

Use the Property Inspector to adjust the size of the AP element to 100 pixels wide by 60 pixels high. We only want this box to be small as it's going to be used for our thumbnail:

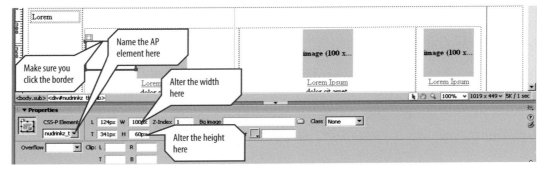

Figure 3.8

Notice that once you click off it, the AP element immediately changes to the new size.

 Name the AP element:

nudrinkz_thumb

 Now we need to create another AP element in the same way, but this time it will be used for the large image so the size should be set at 500 pixels wide by 300 pixels high. Position the new AP element where you want the larger image to appear on the page – in this case to the right of the thumbnail box so that it doesn't overlap with the one you have just made.

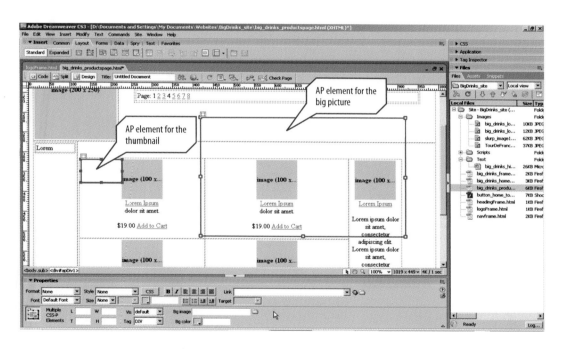

Figure 3.9

Now you can insert the images into their AP elements:

 Click *inside* the 'thumbnail' AP element to highlight it – it will turn blue when it is highlighted.

Click the **Common** tab on the **Insert** toolbar.

 Click the drop-down box next to the Image icon and choose the **Image** button as in Figure 3.10.

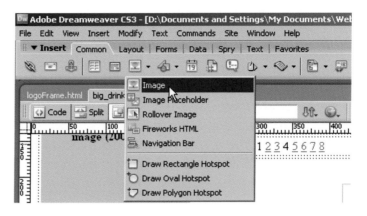

Figure 3.10

 Use the **Select Image Source** dialogue box to navigate to the folder where the nudrinkz_thumb.jpg file that you downloaded at the start of this task is kept on your system.

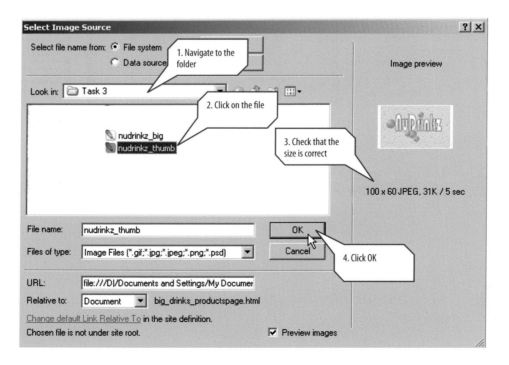

Figure 3.11

16 When you have located the file, click on it and then click **OK**.

A warning appears telling you that the image file is not in the root folder for the website and it offers to make a copy for you in the root folder. Remember – only those files in your root folder will be recognised when you view your website in the browser so:

Figure 3.12

17 … Click **Yes**!

Great, that saves some work!

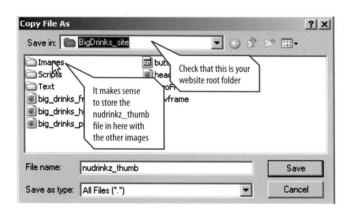

Figure 3.13

18 Type '**nudrinkz_thumb**' into the **Image Tag Accessibility Attributes** dialogue box:

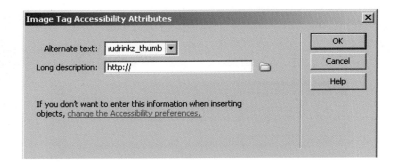

Figure 3.14

19 Click **OK**.

20 The thumbnail now appears in the AP element:

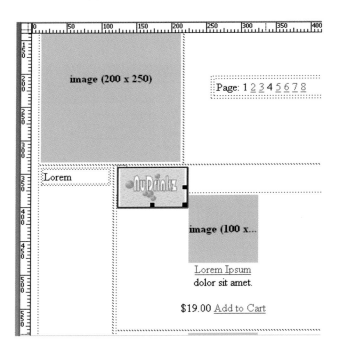

Figure 3.15

21 The process is just the same for the large image, which is saved as:

nudrinkz_big

Use this name also to label the AP element and the Image Tag Accessibility Attributes.

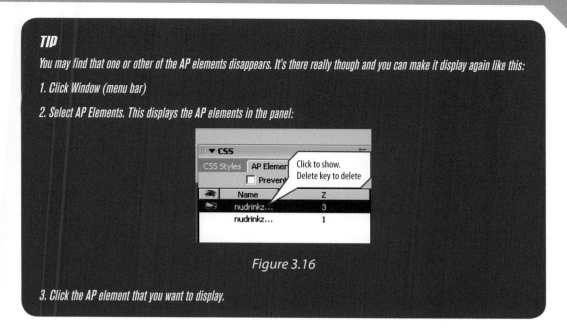
Your screen should now look like this:

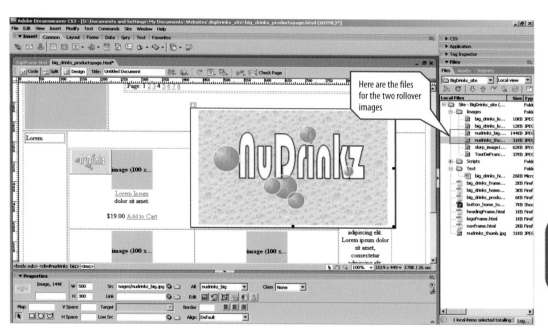

Figure 3.17

Once you have inserted both images into their AP elements, the next job is to make them appear and disappear when you roll over them. This involves three settings:

➤ Setting properties.

➤ Setting behaviours.

➤ Setting events.

PROPERTIES

 22 Select the nudrinkz_big element by clicking the *border* of the element:

Figure 3.18

 23 Change the **Vis** (visibility) property to **Hidden**.

BEHAVIOURS

We have set the Vis property of the large image to Hidden because it won't be visible until you roll over the thumbnail. However we now need to tell the program that we want it to become visible again at some point (i.e. when rolled over) so that's what we will do next. You use the behaviour settings to do this.

 24 Click **Windows** on the menu bar and select **Behaviors**:

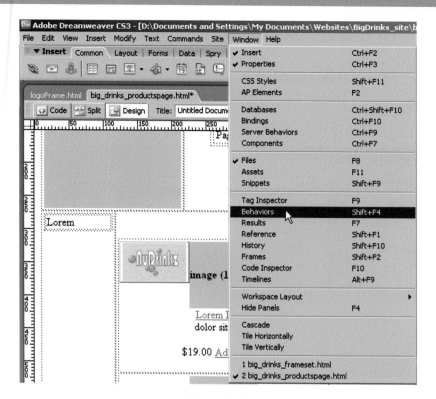

Figure 3.19

25 Select the nudrinkz_thumb AP element by clicking on its border.

26 Click the **Add Behavior** button in the **Attributes** panel on the right of the screen:

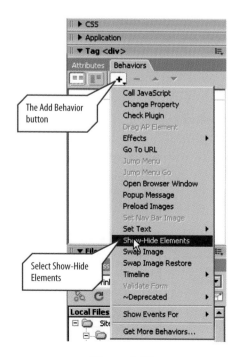

Figure 3.20

27 Click on the **Show-Hide Elements** button in the shortcut list.

28 In the **Show-Hide Elements** dialogue box select:

div "nudrinkz_big"

Figure 3.21

29 Click **Show**.

30 Click **OK**.

EVENTS

Now that we have set what will happen, that is the large image will become visible again, we now need to set which *event* will cause it to become visible – in this case it will be when the thumbnail is rolled over. There are many different events to choose from but we are going to use the 'onMouseOver' event.

31 Click the **onFocus** button to display the list of events.

32 Select the **onMouseOver** event from the drop-down list:

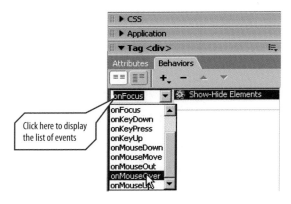

Figure 3.22

We have now set the behaviour 'Show' to occur when the mouse pointer is over the thumbnail.

However, we need to add another event. This time the event will be **onMouseOut**, which means when the mouse pointer is removed from over the thumbnail. We are going to use this event to cause the Behavior 'Hide' to make the large image disappear again.

 Click the **Add Behaviors** button (see Figure 3.20).

 Select (click) **Show-Hide Elements** from the drop-down list.

 Click div 'nudrinkz_big' and then the **Hide** button.

 Click **OK**.

The new event will appear as an **onFocus** event at the top of the list of events, so click on **onFocus** and change it by selecting **onMouseOut** from the drop-down list.

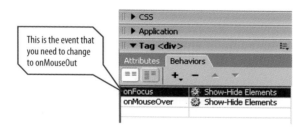

Figure 3.23

Now try the page out!

 Click the **Preview/Debug** button on the **Document** toolbar.

 Select your browser from the list.

 When the **Save** option appears, click **Yes**.

Figure 3.24

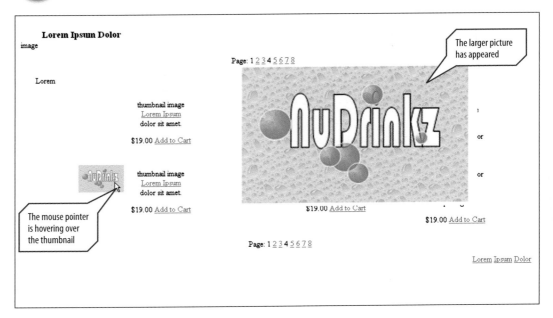

Figure 3.25

So the images now operate correctly, but can we make them more informative for our audience?

The images show the packaging style and the font that will be used on the new range of drinks, but they don't tell you anything about the drinks themselves, so how can customers make a choice about whether to order them or not? Let's add some more information.

What do customers need to know before they make a decision about whether to buy the new range of drinks?

Remember – the customers using this website are shop managers so the information they'll need is likely to be:

> The type of customer the drinks range is aimed at – in this case it's athletes or people who exercise regularly.

> The benefits of the drinks so that the shops can use this in their advertising to attract the right customers – in this case it's that they provide energy over a long time.

> The ingredients of the drinks so that the shops can inform their customers what they will be drinking – for instance it might be important to state that a drink is sugar free.

So let's add some information…

What we need is something like Figure 3.26.

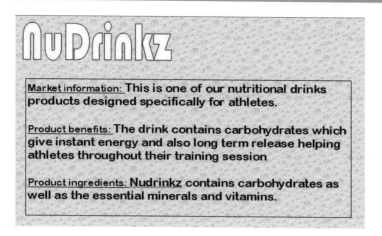

Figure 3.26

This would appear on the web page only if the user was interested in finding further information about the product. Rather than the information automatically showing when the mouse is rolled over the thumbnail, we are going to instruct the program only to show the information if the thumbnail is clicked on.

We can do this using a similar method to the rollover images.

 Draw another AP element and place it above the thumbnail AP element. This time set the size in the Property Inspector to 300 pixels wide and 200 pixels high.

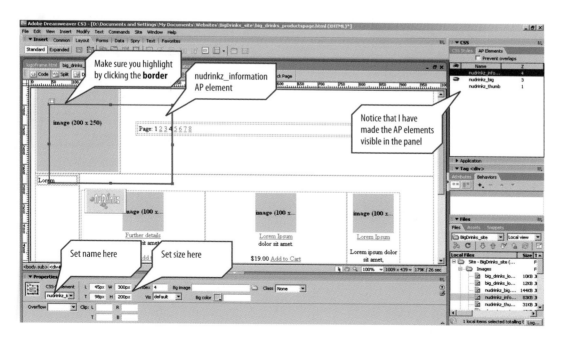

Figure 3.27

Use the **Image** button to copy the file named

Nudrinkz_information.jpg

into your Big Drinks website Images folder and into the new AP element. You may want to review Figures 3.10–3.14 to remind yourself how this is done.

 Highlight the new AP element and use the **Property Inspector** to set its **Vis** property to **Hidden**.

You now need to make a new behaviour for the nudrinkz_thumb AP element. Just as before, it needs to make something appear, but this time it is the nudrinkz_information AP element that is to appear so follow the instructions as shown in Figure 3.28.

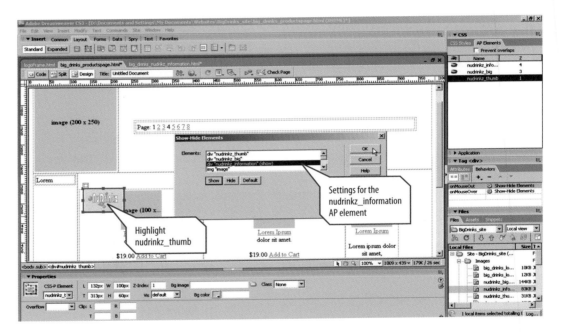

Figure 3.28

44 Click **OK**.

45 Change the **onFocus** event to **onClick**:

Figure 3.29

So far we have set the behaviour for the appearance of the information AP element. We now have to make it disappear!

It would make sense if the user just clicked the information to cause it to close – the same as they have to do to open it – so let's do this next:

46 Make the nudrinkz_information AP element visible using the panel (see the Tip on page 87).

47 Click the border.

48 Set a new behaviour.

FUNCTIONAL SKILLS

When you create websites you always have to think about your audience – not only about the information you are putting on the pages, but also about the way they are able to access the information. We can call this the user experience. For instance, you should make it as easy as possible to find information, because people will get bored looking for it if there are too many clicks through to different pages or if the navigation buttons are not well labelled. You don't want to lose sales just because you have designed a website that is difficult to use!

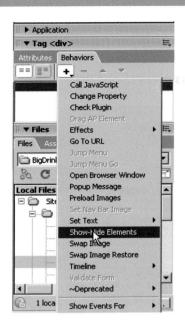

Figure 3.30

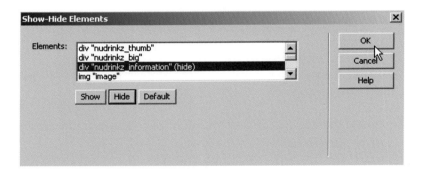

Figure 3.31

 Set an **onClick** event to trigger the behaviour, so that clicking the information will cause it to close.

Figure 3.32

50 Try it out! A good way to test the site is to load it and let a friend try it out. They'll find faults that you don't see any more because you've looked at it so many times!

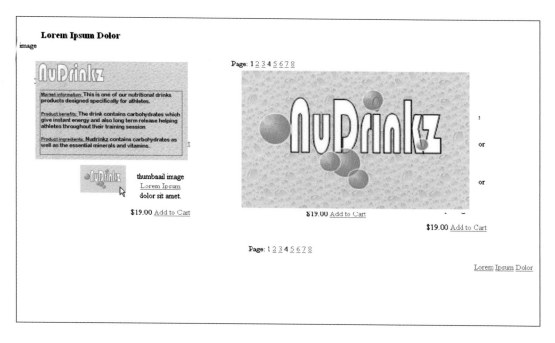

Figure 3.33

That's it!

GET AHEAD

There is a lot of tidying that you could do – here are a few ideas to get you started:

➤ There is only one product in the products page. You could add others – why not add Slurp and provide a link to its web page from the products page?

➤ The grey boxes on the products page are image placeholders. You could put images for other products into these and delete the ones that you don't need.

➤ You could add the Big Drinks logo to the products and Slurp pages.

➤ What about changing the background colours to the blue and green used by Big Drinks? Do you remember how you did this in Task 2?

➤ You could add another sporting picture to one of the pages, such as the Slurp page, and also some information about the drink.

➤ You will probably need to delete some more items not needed on the Slurp and products pages.

➤ Try out some different font styles – but remember, this is a website designed for other users and not just to please your own tastes!

➤ Swap to the Forms tab on the Insert toolbar and use the Text Field control ⬚ to add a space for donations to the 'Everest Base Camp Cleanup' (see Figure 3.34). You can add a check box too!

➤ Make a 'Contact Us' section and insert an email link ⬚ (the button for this is in the Common tab). When you load the site into your web browser, you can click the link and an email form pops up – magic!

Here are some of the effects that are possible:

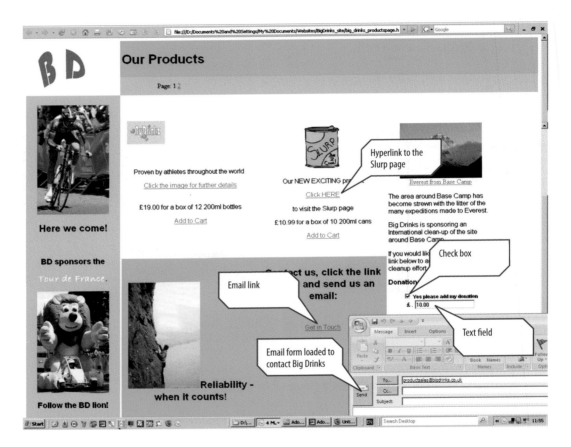

Figure 3.34

Revising the skills that you have learnt by tackling some of these ideas will be useful because the next activity is the Project, where you will not have the support of being told how to do the techniques.

CHECKPOINT

Check that you know how to:

➤ Zoom in and out to aid editing.

➤ Insert rollover buttons.

➤ Add and resize AP elements.

➤ Insert an image into an AP element.

➤ Change the size, name and visibility properties of AP elements.

➤ Use behaviours.

➤ Use events to start a behaviour.

➤ Thoroughly test a website during development.

ASSESSMENT POINT

Now let's assess the work. Look back at the table at the beginning of this section (**Target point**) and decide on which of the statements you can answer 'Yes' to.

Did you do as well as you expected? Could you improve your work? Use Word to write a comment to show what you could do to improve your work and remember this when starting your next ICT project.

The Project

BYTES 4 BITES

TASK BRIEF

The theme for the project is a website for the new 'Break Bites' break-time ordering system run by the sixth form.
You have just received this email:

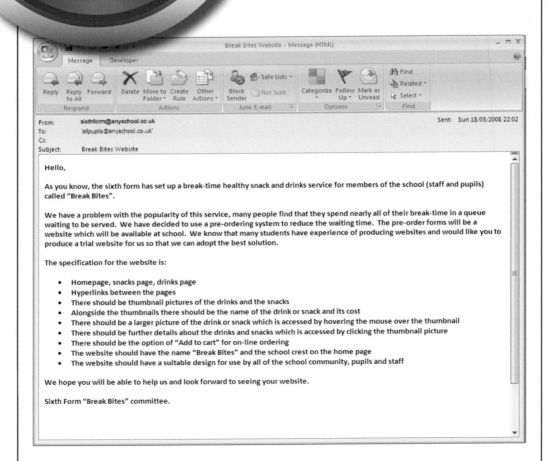

Break Bites Website - Message (HTML)

Message   Developer

Reply | Reply to All | Forward | Delete | Move to Folder | Create Rule | Other Actions | Block Sender | Safe Lists | Not Junk | Categorize | Follow Up | Mark as Unread | Find | Related | Select

Respond | Actions | Junk E-mail | Options | Find

From: sixthform@anyschool.co.uk
To: 'allpupils@anyschool.co.uk'
Cc:
Subject: Break Bites Website

Sent: Sun 18/05/2008 22:02

Hello,

As you know, the sixth form has set up a break-time healthy snack and drinks service for members of the school (staff and pupils) called "Break Bites".

We have a problem with the popularity of this service, many people find that they spend nearly all of their break-time in a queue waiting to be served. We have decided to use a pre-ordering system to reduce the waiting time. The pre-order forms will be a website which will be available at school. We know that many students have experience of producing websites and would like you to produce a trial website for us so that we can adopt the best solution.

The specification for the website is:

- Homepage, snacks page, drinks page
- Hyperlinks between the pages
- There should be thumbnail pictures of the drinks and the snacks
- Alongside the thumbnails there should be the name of the drink or snack and its cost
- There should be a larger picture of the drink or snack which is accessed by hovering the mouse over the thumbnail
- There should be further details about the drinks and snacks which is accessed by clicking the thumbnail picture
- There should be the option of "Add to cart" for on-line ordering
- The website should have the name "Break Bites" and the school crest on the home page
- The website should have a suitable design for use by all of the school community, pupils and staff

We hope you will be able to help us and look forward to seeing your website.

Sixth Form "Break Bites" committee.

Figure Project.1

You should produce a website to meet the specification given in the above email.

To meet this project brief you need to complete the website, paying attention to all of the requirements set out in the email above. Remember, part of your job is to test the functionality of the website, so check that it loads correctly in a number of different web browsers as well as testing all of the links and making sure that the rollover images work correctly.

Think of the audience when you are designing the website; some of them will be members of staff, so the website should appeal to them as well as to pupils in the school.

The "Suggested way of working" section below shows how you could cover the specification and maximise your level and marks from the project. It is important to plan the project at the outset, but don't feel that the plan restricts what you do later; very often better ways of working occur to you during the design process and, if these fit with the brief, you should adopt the better ideas even though they do not occur in the original plan. You can comment on the changes to the original plan in the evaluation section.

The Functional Skills listed below show you the skills you will be demonstrating in your work but remember you have to know WHY you have chosen to demonstrate them in a particular way and how your choice match you audience and purpose for the documents.

> Planning your website.

> Using suitable software.

> Saving files in the root folder of the website using suitable filenames.

> Using a suitable template and web page layout.

> Editing text and backgrounds with suitable fonts, colours and styles.

> Inserting and editing images (cropping images to size, making rollovers).

> Linking pages using hyperlinks.

> Testing the functionality of the website.

> Evaluating the effectiveness of the website as a solution to the problem outlined in the brief.

ASSESSMENT OBJECTIVES

TARGET POINT

Have a look at the following statements before you start your task so you know what you are aiming for.

Level 3	Level 4	Level 5	Level 6
You have made a list of the items need for the website and placed them in an appropriate order	You have broken down tasks (for example, you have made a list of assets needed)	You have found suitable assets needed for the task and identified any changes needed	You have identified the needs of the pupils and staff who will use the website
You have gathered assets together and stored files in folders	You have made new folders within the root folder for different assets (for example, a folder for images)		
You have used structures such as frames to divide pages in your website	You have successfully set up frames in the website	You have suitably arranged the information in structures such as frames or tables	You have arranged information logically, showing you understand how pupils and staff will use the website.
You have inserted text or an image	You have inserted relevant text or images	You have inserted relevant text and images from several sources	You have changed or combined images to make the result more suitable for the target audience
You have used a hyperlink	You have inserted a hyperlink in your website	You have added hyperlinks to enable the user to move from page to page in your website	You have added links so that users can move freely from any page to another within the website
You have improved the layout by using formatting (e.g. fonts, background)	You have made extensive use of formatting	You have used formatting throughout your website to make the site more suitable for its intended users	Your plan clearly shows how you intend to make your website suitable for use by both pupils and staff
You have tested a hyperlink	You have performed a test to make sure that the website loads correctly into a web browser. You have checked that a hyperlink opens the correct page	You understand why the tests are necessary and you have carried out tests in more than one browser	You have successfully tested the whole project by trialling with the target users. You have reacted systematically to any problems resulting from testing

SUGGESTED WAY OF WORKING

Item	What you could do	What it will look like
Make a plan	Use planning software	A 'spider diagram' to show the different pages need for the website. The diagram could also show what each page will contain and how it will be used by pupils and staff
	Make a list	A list of 'assets' (pictures, writing, etc.) that will be needed for the website
		A list of software that you will need to complete the task. Give a use for each piece of software
	Estimate time	A table to show estimates for how long each item of the project will take to complete
	Think about how pupils and staff will use the website	A table to show how pupils and staff will use the pages and controls of the website
Make a layout	Use templates to make the pages of the website.	Preformed web pages that have a suitable layout for the Break Bites website
	Add Hyperlinks (use buttons) to link the pages.	A home page with links to other pages (one will be used for ordering snacks, another for ordering drinks)
Format the pages	Delete items not needed.	Clearer design
	Change fonts	Clear and readable headings to pages
	Change backgrounds	
	Make rollover images	Rollovers display thumbnails and details of snacks and drinks
	Change function (e.g. change the properties of form controls so that users can record their order on the website)	Form controls such as checkboxes for users to record their order
		A submit button ('Add to cart') for users to place their order
Test the website	Load the website into different web browsers	Check that the website appears correctly
	Check hyperlinks between pages	Correctly labelled buttons that function as would be expected
	Check rollover images	The thumbnail image is replaced by a larger image (e.g. of food sold by Break Bites)
Evaluate the project	Compare the specification of the brief to your final website	A table or text to show your comments on the differences and give reasons why these have occurred
	Compare your original plan to your final website	A table or text to show your comments on the differences and give reasons why these have occurred

Now it's your turn!

INDEX